PRAISE FOR
SCIENCE OF A HAPPY BRAIN

"*Science of a Happy Brain* brings up several issues that both plague our society and provide hope for the future. In our modern society, which seemingly provides everything that one would believe one needs, isolation and despair seem to rule. Dr. Jay Kumar gives some tantalizing thoughts, based on novel science results, and makes the case that our happy brains might be the answer to both personal and societal issues that seem too complex to tackle."

—**Deepak Chopra M.D., FACP**, is a world-renowned pioneer in integrative medicine and personal transformation, and has published a large number of books, many of them *New York Times* bestsellers.

"In his inspiring new book, *Science of a Happy Brain*, Dr. Jay offers a fresh perspective on the age-old quest for happiness and shows us how to move from a *despairing brain* to a *Happy Brain*. He explains why the *disease of despair* has risen to epic proportions, while pointing out how anger, anxiety, addiction, isolation, depression, disconnection, stress (and more) are hijacking our happiness. But he also offers hope and guidance, along with ways to understand the inner workings of our brains—urging us not just to survive, but to thrive. *Science of a Happy Brain* is rich with wisdom and hard science, blended together and carefully explained so non-scientific minds can grasp. Dr. Jay shares a life-changing trauma that led him into despair and also shares how it inspired him to take on his life's mission for helping people create happiness. Perhaps one of the most important questions he poses is: What is happiness to you? Answering that question gives you a running start in discovering the secret to your Happy Brain that he relays in his book."

—**Lexie Brockway Potamkin**
Author, *What Is Spirit?*

"*Science of a Happy Brain* is contextually framed by recent advances in social neuroscience; a field that has provided integrated insights into the neurobiological pathways that contribute to the salutary effects of social relationships on psychological and physical health. Drawing upon personal events and shared stories, as well as broad cultural and religious perspectives, Dr. Jay Kumar brings to life the scientific links between social connections and psychological well-being, and provides strategies with the goal for fostering gratitude, kindness, and compassion toward the development of happiness discovered in meaningful attachments to others and to causes larger than ourselves."

—**Michael R. Irwin, M.D.**
Cousins Distinguished Professor of Psychiatry and Biobehavioral Sciences, David Geffen School of Medicine at UCLA
Distinguished Professor of Psychology, UCLA
College of Letters and Sciences
Director, Cousins Center for Psychoneuroimmunology
Director, Mindful Awareness Research Center
Jane and Terry Semel Institute for Neuroscience and Human Behavior at UCLA

"*Science of a Happy Brain* outlines valuable lessons each and every one of us can learn about the biological, psychological, social, and spiritual evolution of the human brain. From the Stone Age to the Present Age, Dr. Jay unleashes the antidote to anger, anxiety, addiction, and the worst culprit of all—social isolation. Via the marriage of science and spirituality, Dr. Jay reinforces the key factors that result in healthy interactions—the need for value, the need for belonging, and the need for engagement. This book is a must keep on your nightstand to read and reread every time your brain reverts back to the survival brain your ancestors had back in the Stone Age. The end result, a happy brain equals happy people equals a happy world. I would highly recommend anyone and everyone to take Dr. Jay's Happiness course!"

—Arica Hilton
President at Hilton Asmus Contemporary

"There are certainly many books on happiness that one can find in the market. But rare is a book that makes sense both scientifically and socially. *Science of a Happy Brain* by Dr. Jay Kumar addresses issues of immediate concern to our modern society and individual human beings making up all societies. He makes the case that bringing back long-forgotten aspects of our core humanity is very much needed. Working from scientific findings and coupled with years of experience from teaching in the subject, Dr. Jay Kumar eloquently makes the case of an undeniable truth—*to socialize is to survive, to tribe is to thrive.* Bringing in his own perspective and experience with life's challenges, makes the book a warm, human testimony, beyond just a strong academic work. His thesis and practical steps all provide hope that a better future is indeed our birthright—in congruence with our happy brains—pointing to a bright future for society as well."

—Menas C. Kafatos is the Fletcher Jones Endowed Professor of Computational Physics at Chapman University. He is the coauthor of *The Conscious Universe* (Springer), coauthor with Deepak Chopra of *The New York Times* bestseller *You Are the Universe* (Harmony), and author of *Living the Living Presence* in Korean and Greek.

"In this empowering work—drawn from his personal experience, self-reflection, and growth—Dr. Jay offers a simple and clear road map to understanding and applying strategies that will help you identify and build your Happy Brain. *Science of a Happy Brain* is guaranteed to grab you intellectually, touch you emotionally, and awaken you spiritually while deepening your connection and communication with yourself, your family, and the society that you live in. A must read for every parent who wants to raise children to thrive."

—Roma Khetarpal
Founder of *Tools of Growth*
Educator and author of the award-winning book,
The "Perfect" Parent

SCIENCE OF A HAPPY BRAIN

———■———

Thriving in the Age of
Anger, Anxiety, and Addiction

———■———

DR. JAY KUMAR

Your Happiness Professor

Happy brains make happy people.
Happy people make a happy world.

PAGE PUBLISHING, INC.
Conneaut Lake, PA

First originally published by Page Publishing 2019

ISBN 978-1-64462-801-0 (pbk)
ISBN 978-1-64462-802-7 (digital)

Printed in the United States of America

This book is dedicated to the loving memory of my mother and to all those who seek the tools and wisdom for achieving your Happy Brain.

Contents

ACKNOWLEDGMENTS

The extent of gratitude I owe to the following people, who've made *Science of a Happy Brain* a reality, are numerous and diverse. No matter which "tribe" you represent in my life, each of you, in your special way, supported me on this journey when I've required it the most. Most of all, you continue to be the source of my "Happy Brain," now and always. I recognize and honor:

- My Family Tribe—in enduring memory to my mom and with profound reverence to my dad, both of whose support and love reside at the heart of this work; tremendous thanks to Sheela, Sandeep, Molly, Kris, Peggy, and all the Shepardsons; to my extended Kumar and Nadkarny clans spread out across the globe; and to my lifelong connection to the Hemmady, Amladi, Goel, Panwalker, and Shenoy families.

- My ABSRI Tribe—with genuine gratitude to Paul Tobin, Arun Abey, Bernie Bolger, Greg French, Michael Gardiner, Lori Brown, Rory McCracken, Tom Martin, Abbie Britton, Caitlin Ruderman, Julia Kasza, Alex Godinez, and Richard Mark, for your expertise and encouragement in every phase of this complex process. A special note of thanks to George Hampton and everyone at the law firm of Hampton Holley, for the generous use of their conference room and office space while conducting research for this book.

- My Academic Tribe—with deep esteem to Dr. Gail Stearns, Dr. Menas C. Kafatos, Dr. Susan Yang, Dr. Michael Irwin, Dr. Vijay Sathe, Dr. Benjamin Rosenberg, Dr. Louis Cozolino, Dr. Gurucharan Singh Khalsa, Dr. Gopal

Shenoy, Dr. Sallie Smith, and Dr. Julie Brown Yau for your insights and inspiration; to all my teachers, professors, and mentors who've nurtured my passion for education; and to all my students over the decades who grant me the opportunity to share my message with such joy.

- My Writers Tribe—in profound honor to Dr. Deepak Chopra, Lexie Brockway Potamkin, Gopi Kallayil, Arica Hilton, and Roma Kheterpal, for your praise and prose to this project.

- My Soul Tribe—with heartfelt admiration to Darci Frankel, Elsa Flores Almaraz, Dixie and Martin Van der Kamp, Serena Carroll, Samantha Terhune, Lisa La Joie, Christine Coppola, Bob Richter, Rita Connor, Lynne LaBorde Eastman, and Vanessa Simpkins, for your unwavering faith and spiritual guidance throughout this journey.

- My Friends Tribe—with powerful respect to Don Zyck, Christine Sisley, Ken Garen, Steve Smith, Steve Stella, Elysabeth Alfano, Ken Kornbluh, Julie and Shawn Glanville, Christopher Krywulak, Zella and Larry Cox, T.J. Campbell, David Gaydos, Ilakshi Patel, Reshma Patel, Heike and Richard Wells, Brad Ray, David Dahlin, Frank Brooks, Doug Stephan, and everyone at "Doug Stephan's Good Day" radio show, for your unwavering encouragement and support. I owe a special recognition to Brian Mutert and Derek Perrigo, for allowing me to finalize the edits of this book's manuscript in the serenity and solitude of their Sonoma Mountain guesthouse.

- My Publishing Tribe—with tremendous thanks to Diana Botteon, David Rodax, Nick Hoffman, and to all the editors at Page Publishing, for birthing this book from its inception into final form.

FOREWORD

The Happy Human Meets the Happiness Professor

I first met Dr. Jay outside baggage claim at Orange County's John Wayne airport in Southern California. He pulled up to the curb in his bright red Mini Cooper, flashing his equally bright smile, looking less like a college professor and more like an enthusiastic, cheerful sales executive for a software company. He'd invited me to speak to the students in his extremely popular Happiness course at Chapman University and was here to drive me to campus. I was excited to be in the Southern California sunshine and intrigued to meet this man who'd been given the title the "Happiness Professor." (After all, I carried in my wallet personal cards that read "The Happy Human.")

As we drove on the freeway to Chapman, talking about our work and our lives, I was struck by this extremely articulate, erudite scholar's earnestness, his sense of ordinariness and humility. These qualities—that make Dr. Jay so engaging—inform every page of *Science of a Happy Brain*. His science-based elements and strategies for your Happy Brain, taught in his course, are clear, compelling, and, in our increasingly disconnected world, necessary. I was captivated from the first page, caught by how he bridged the scientific and spiritual with ease. I can see why his class is in such demand. During our time together, I simply warmed to him, felt very comfortable with him, connected with his spiritual awareness—very similar to my own—and, of course, his Indian origin. We are of the same tribe.

What is it about happiness? Why are we so obsessed? The subject of happiness has fueled a multimillion-dollar industry. My Google search for "books on happiness" yielded 439,000,000 results. It seems every public personality has a book on happiness, including the Pope

(*Happiness in this Life*) and the Dalai Lama (*The Art of Happiness*). Bhutan and the United Arab Emirates have ministers dedicated to happiness. There's even a World Happiness Report, which ranks 126 countries on their happiness quotient. Across cultures and across countries, happiness is one of the most researched, talked-about topics. And there's a reason for all this. Happiness is one of the most fundamental and unique needs of humanity. Everyone wants to be happy. It doesn't matter which country, or what segment of society. As the fourteenth Dalai Lama—to me, the true embodiment of happiness—has said, "Like oneself, all other sentient beings are equal in having this wish to be happy and to overcome suffering."

A few years ago, I had the great honor of meeting with His Holiness in Dharamshala, India. Here, was this person who had none of the conventional trappings or markers of what we consider would lead to happiness. He has no money; as a monk, he's not supposed to keep any. He has no country; he was forced to flee Tibet when he was twenty-three, exactly sixty years ago, in 1959. And yet, when you meet him, there's this sense of excitement, this mirth, a bubbling up of happiness and joy that comes from within him. I find it so intriguing that happiness may come from sources that differ from what, traditionally, humans have considered yield happiness.

Currently, much of our pursuit of happiness is focused on the next best thing out there. We change our job, our partner, our city, our car—hoping they will lead to happiness. But as the teachers of all the ages have repeatedly told us, "You can only find happiness from within, and from shifting your consciousness." My understanding of happiness is derived from my own cultural and spiritual traditions, stemming from Indian philosophy, which alludes to the notions of existential searching and of *sat-chit-ananda*, the idea that we are existence, knowledge, and bliss absolute, and if we look long enough within, we unearth these truths. Conversely, as long as we look outside, and keep crashing around and searching around and living this frenzied life, we're not going to find that state of enlightened bliss.

One of the reasons I'm so fascinated by Dr. Jay's scientific approach to happiness and the work he's doing at his Applied Brain

Science Research Institute is that his Four Elements of a Happy Brain—biological, psychological, social, and spiritual—make no mention of material possessions. I couldn't help thinking that this model might explain the Dalai Lama's happiness.

Wisdom traditions have also looked at happiness through the lens of these elements. From a biological aspect, they speak to the importance of breath, movement, and food. From a psychological perspective, they encourage practices, like music, meditation, and mindfulness. When it comes to social connection, these wisdom traditions build solidarity and encourage community-based gatherings, where prayer and meditation are practiced. And then, there's the spiritual dimension of happiness, coming from a sense of contact with a consciousness that is larger than we are—a consciousness that encompasses us all.

In essence, Dr. Jay, one of the foremost researchers in the science of happiness, has taken what the ancient traditions knew to be true, incorporated his work on the science of a Happy Brain and created a strategy for how each of us can find happiness in its deepest sense. At the same time, he has had to surrender to the fact that, at the end of the day, even with all the scientific evidence of what constitutes a Happy Brain, the spiritual traditions really knew a thing or two about happiness.

These wisdom traditions did not arrive at these conclusions simply by constructing complex, archaic, esoteric theories. They arrived at them by trial-and-error, testing practices and methods on themselves. The Buddha discovered this path to inner peace and the liberation from suffering by observing his mind and by experimenting with his mental data and his breath. Unfortunately, at that time—sixth to fifth century BCE—the Buddha didn't have access to the neurotechnology we have today, so he didn't have a scientific leg to stand on. All he had was the power of observation.

And today, that's not enough. We live in a world where, unless results are scientifically proven, measured in our body, brain, and mind, many people are hesitant to embrace this ancient wisdom. And this is where the work that Dr. Jay has done—his belief that the "convergence between empirical scientific knowledge and experiential spiritual wisdom is a valid mode of revelation"—is so ground-breaking. Think of the people his work can reach—all those who need hard facts before they believe. Think of the healing—the shift from disconnection and despair toward connection, meaningful contribution, and happiness. Do we need another book on happiness? We need this one.

Navigating Your "Inner-Net"

Recently, I was presenting at the second Annual World Happiness Summit, where Dr. Fred Luskin was also a speaker. Fred is the Director of the Stanford Forgiveness Project and three-time author. Fred made us do an exercise. He said our mind naturally focuses on grudges, the people who've hurt us, and the things that have upset us. It's the nature of our mind. Our minds just linger around these constructs. But we don't ask, "Who has been kind to me in the last twenty-four hours?" "Who has been kind to me?" Fred asked us to shift our attention and to think of ten people who've been kind to us, whether we asked for it or not, of their own volition. He asked us to watch how doing so changes our state of happiness.

That peak state is the portal to fulfillment and happiness that comes from sharing expressions of kindness and compassion—making eye contact and saying "Hello" or "Thank you" to the TSA agent, the person at the dishwashing station at your school cafeteria, or the new intern at work. That simple human connection will uplift you. It will uplift others.

Fred's exercise speaks to the science of a Happy Brain that Dr. Jay writes about. To make yourself and others happy, you need to recognize, acknowledge, and appreciate them for their value and worth.

As Chief Evangelist of Digital Marketing at Google, I often speak and write about how to integrate our inner and outer technologies in a screen-crazed, hyper-connected world. Ultimately, we can only experience happiness through our own container: our body, our brain, and our breath. What I call affectionately, our inner-net. We bear responsibility for our inner-net—keeping it in peak performance. Others may guide us, mentor us, coach us, but keeping our inner-net in optimal condition is on us. Every bit of this life experience is being filtered, processed, and interpreted by this system. All our life expressions are outputs of our inner-net. Any expression of creativity, productivity, expression that impacts others, the world—all come from this place.

So it's logical to conclude that the quality of our life is determined by the quality of our inner-net. If we put this complex system into a state of peak performance, we experience life at a peak state. We express ourselves at a peak state, sharing our innate gifts and talents—whatever they may be.

While *Science of a Happy Brain* is a highly useful and revolutionary tool, the important thing is to read it, study it, understand it, and then *take action*—experiment. Experiment with the scientifically-validated concepts in these pages. Try these exercises in your own life, and observe yourself, as the Buddha did. As I've learned from my years attending Burning Man, all of life is one giant experiment. Experiments lead to unexpected, often brilliant results, but you will never find out until you try.

I wish you the very best on your own journey and pathway to happiness as you explore the incredible amount of information and wisdom in *Science of a Happy Brain*. Experiment, and eventually declare yourself to be the Happy Human, worthy of being a student of the Happiness Professor.

—Gopi Kallayil
June 10, 2019

Gopi Kallayil is Chief Evangelist, Digital Marketing at Google. In his prior roles at Google, he led the marketing team for the company's flagship advertising product, AdWords, both in the Americas and Asia Pacific, and headed the marketing team for AdSense, Google's publisher-facing product. He has also led large information technology projects for global corporations in India, China, and the United States. Gopi earned his bachelor's degree in electronics engineering from the National Institute of Technology in India. He received two master's degrees in business administration—

one from the Indian Institute of Management and another from The Wharton School of Business at the University of Pennsylvania.

In addition to being an avid yoga practitioner and teacher, Gopi is a triathlete, public speaker, global traveler, and Burning Man devotee. He has spoken at TEDx, Renaissance Weekend, The World Peace Festival, and Wisdom 2.0, and hosts a TV program on cable and YouTube called *Change Makers*. He is the author of two books, *The Happy Human* and *The Internet to the Inner-net*, published by Hay House. He has released two music albums titled *Kirtan Lounge*. Gopi holds a guest faculty position, teaching brand marketing at the Stanford University Graduate School of Business. He also sits on the Board of Directors of the Desmond Tutu Peace Foundation.

INTRODUCTION

CONFESSIONS FROM A HAPPINESS PROFESSOR

> The wound is the place where the Light enters you.
>
> —Rumi

It was a July evening, and I was relaxing in my studio apartment in Los Angeles enjoying the balmy weather. I just completed the first year in my PhD program at UCLA and was relishing a quiet night alone at home. It was the perfect antidote for having completed an arduous academic year that ended just a month before. The TV was on, and I was making dinner in the kitchen.

The phone rang, and something beyond rational explanation occurred. I heard an alarming voice in my head that clearly warned *This is going to be bad. Get ready for your life to change!*

My first reaction was *Where the hell did that come from?* Whether you attribute it to intuition or imagination, sure enough, to this very day, I swear to having heard that premonition distinctly in my head the moment of the first ring from the phone that evening. I still get the chills thinking about it today.

I was seized with dread from the ominous warning I just received. The phone kept ringing, but I was literally immobile. My hands—that were chopping vegetables—trembled. I couldn't seem to take the five steps to walk over to pick up the phone. I just couldn't shake the cautionary message I just heard in my mind.

After a few more rings, the answering machine went off. A couple of seconds later, I heard the voice of Dad on the line. This immediately struck me as being quite odd. It was always Mom, rarely ever Dad, who made the effort to call me out of the blue. What made his message all the more alarming was the palpable angst and turmoil I could hear in his voice the moment he began speaking on the machine.

"It's Dad here," his voice shaking with hesitation. "Something really bad just happened to Mom." The seriousness and urgency from hearing Dad's voice shook me out of my stupor. I immediately dropped the cutting knife in my hand and raced to the phone.

"Dad, I'm here! What's wrong?" There was a heavy pause. "Dad?" I uttered again apprehensively. I could feel Dad searching for the right words. His thirty years of being a seasoned physician must have instinctively kicked in, and I'm sure he was mustering up his reserve to respond as calmly as possible from his decades of medical training.

"Mom just got taken to the emergency room. The ambulance just left, and I'm calling from home before driving to the hospital."

Before he could continue, I felt a knot tighten in the pit of my stomach. My voice filled with panic. "Wait, what happened? What's wrong? Tell me!" Another few tense seconds of silence passed.

"I came home from work and found her passed out upstairs on the hallway carpet. Mom must have accidentally taken too many pills. I tried to wake her. Her pulse and breath were weak. She was unresponsive and frothing at the mouth. I called 911."

"I'm not understanding!" I responded in confusion, as my legs buckled and my body collapsed on the sofa.

I tried to say something, but Dad interjected, "You need to fly home right away. It's serious. I need to get to the hospital now! Call your brother and tell him to come home. You both need to be in Chicago by the morning. I'll call once I know more."

Before I could even articulate a response, the phone hung up. I sat on the sofa for the next minute dazed and numb, trying my best to catch my breath and to wrap my head around the shock Dad just revealed to me. Although I didn't really require a further explanation from Dad, my instinct already knew the reason why Mom was rushed to ER in an ambulance. The surety of it all hit me like a solid and swift punch to the gut. I replayed the voice I heard in my head less than a minute earlier: *This is going to be bad. Get ready for your life to change!* The revelation from that message was eerily accurate.

My mother had just attempted suicide. My entire being knew it the moment I hung up the phone. But I had it confirmed once I flew home to Chicago early next morning. Mom's "accidently taking too many pills" was done deliberately. Mom remained in a coma on full life support for the next three days before she finally passed. The foreboding message I heard on that fateful evening became a reality. It's astonishing how the trajectory of one's life can transform in the blink of an eye. While the entire call with Dad barely lasted a minute, the entirety of my life became permanently altered.

They say to write about what you know. On July 18, 1994, I learned what it truly meant to suffer. I became deeply intimate with loss. My mother—a graceful woman, caring doctor, devoted wife, beloved sister, loving friend, and attentive neighbor—unexpectedly took her own life. The wake of her death left me battling my own depression and anxiety. I struggled to find my way and purpose. I felt confused, lost, and hopeless.

But from the depths of my existential pain, I began to ponder the crucial questions of the human condition. What is the meaning of life? What drives our behavior? What really matters? How can I achieve a life of purpose, value, and resilience? The fundamental question I was asking myself is this: *What is happiness?* It continues to be the driving question of my personal and professional life. It was on the fateful day of Mom's suicide I unknowingly embarked on the journey to answer this very question.

Everything that has transpired in my life since then—intentionally and accidentally—has in some meaningful way led me to create *Science of a Happy Brain.* While the road to recovery was inarguably arduous at times, it taught me more than I could have ever imagined. My loss became the catalyst for my liberation. I now want to share with you what I've learned along the way from my own healing journey and lifelong investigation into the human brain and the patterns of our behavior. I earnestly desire to help you apply the insights I currently co-teach to students in my university Happiness course. I want you to benefit from the techniques advanced to people around the world in my trainings and seminars—to thrive in life by learning the tools for building your Happy Brain. Most of all, I want you to know it's possible.

In case you didn't know, you've just been accepted into the Happiness course. By simply engaging with *Science of a Happy Brain*, you automatically got into the class. The best part is you don't have to be enrolled in college or be one of my university students to benefit from the wisdom and applied strategies you're about to learn over the next ten lessons. Regardless of your educational background, you qualify to be in this Happiness course. Why do I know so? The desire for happiness is universal. Whether you know it or not, you already possess the insights and the capacity to achieve the benefits of your Happy Brain. As your Happiness professor, I'm merely here to help you awaken and apply them into your life. Welcome to your Happiness course. You've earned your spot!

Nearly twenty-five years later, I still feel the heavy burden of Mom's suicide weighing in my heart and the grief I know will never truly go away. It's due to my own despair and subsequent struggles over the years following this calamity why I continue to remain personally invested in my calling. I consider myself to be more than just an advocate for suicide prevention; I'm a powerful voice for happiness promotion.

Mom's suicide remains, without any question, the most traumatic event of my life. But if it weren't for this tragedy, I doubt myself becoming the person, academic, and advocate I am today—one who remains deeply invested to promoting sustainable health and happiness for others. My pain forged the purpose I required to be of service to you and to anyone having ever endured hardship, suffered loss, or felt helpless.

I suppose it comes as no surprise how I eventually became a Happiness professor and researcher in the brain science of happiness. My own healing journey ultimately became the impetus behind co-founding my organization—the Applied Brain Science Research

Institute (ABSRI) in 2015. In my role at ABSRI, a day doesn't pass when I don't think of Mom as I'm advising corporations, training executives, educating mental health care professionals, leading retreats, or appearing on media. Every day I wake up feeling humbled and grateful getting to do what I love—providing you with the opportunity to cultivate your Happy Brain and revealing the tools to prosper in life.

I feel blessed to research and write about brain science and behavioral health. I am also a scholar of Eastern religions and contemplative studies, in addition to holding graduate degrees in politics, economics, philosophy, and linguistics. That said, faith and spirituality are deeply important to me, reflected in my becoming a certified yoga/meditation instructor and a spiritual counselor. All these aspects of my academic, professional, spiritual, and personal life are equally expressed throughout *Science of a Happy Brain*. Neglecting to do so would be disingenuous to who I am.

As your Happiness professor, my role is more than merely to help you acquire the tools for achieving your Happy Brain. Empowering you to overcome anger, anxiety, addiction, PTSD, depression, loneliness, and loss is what drives my passion and brings my life true purpose. What I do is more than just a career; it's my life's calling. From the arduous process of transforming my own anguish into action, I'm granted the opportunity to help you harness the power of your Happy Brain as I myself have done.

Since that life-altering summer evening in 1994, I've been on a quest for happiness. During the nearly twenty-five years following Mom's suicide, I've attended dozens of self-help seminars and retreats, sought spiritual wisdom at the feet of holy gurus in Indian ashrams, and spent years in therapy. I've also read countless books on happiness and viewed numerous TED talks on positive psychology in the self-help genre. But despite the valuable knowledge gained from all of these experiences and many years of soul-searching, they were incapable of healing my core anguish and pain. Something was missing, yet I didn't know what.

It wasn't until my early forties that I had my epiphany. I earnestly began to study brain science and the underlying factors driving human behavior—specifically in the context for healing my own trauma and pain. I came to understand that in order to achieve a Happy Brain, it's important to recognize the various mechanisms evolved in the human brain that express happiness. It's crucial for you to explore the patterns of behavior that simultaneously sabotage and sustain your Happy Brain.

What I've produced here for you is a unique program I've created and synthesized from both timeless spiritual wisdom and recent advances in brain science. It's a model for achieving sustainable happiness that draws the best from two realms of human inquiry—science and spirituality. Better yet, you don't require an advanced degree or any prior background in brain science to benefit from your Happiness course. Nor do you have to be aligned to any specific religion—or even believe in a divine power—to apply the strategies outlined over the next ten lessons into your life. You just have to believe in yourself.

Everything I'm about to share with you in *Science of a Happy Brain* is real—whether affirmed by groundbreaking research in brain science and behavioral health or advanced by universal wisdom from the world's spiritual traditions. You will dive deeply into the secrets behind your brain and explore the mystery of the human condition. More importantly, my intention is to reveal a novel strategy—established in brain science—for you to create a life of balance, longevity, and resilience as the powerful products of your Happy Brain. Your Happy Brain is a healthy brain. Your healthy brain is the key to becoming a happy human. Happy humans create a happy world. It all starts with building your Happy Brain.

So why brain science? Science has revealed more about your brain in the past ten years than in the past one thousand years. You literally, my friends, are living in what I call the "Decade of the Brain." Brain science is an emerging interdisciplinary field that encompasses research from neuroscience, psychology, medicine, and behavioral health. That said, I continue to be amazed how current discoveries in brain science profoundly affirm what timeless spiritual traditions have advanced over millennia—as both providing a complementary perspective into the nature of human suffering and the key to your happiness.

But there's another reason why I remain excited about having you in this Happiness course. Brain science is revolutionizing the existing medical model of disease, depression, trauma, addiction, anxiety, and even what sabotages your happiness. In the training seminars I provide to mental health care professionals, I frame the construct of suffering and happiness via the emerging *Bio-Psycho-Socio-Spiritual model* of illness and health. Allow me to introduce what this very important concept means.

For the past few centuries, Western (allopathic) medicine has conceptualized the cause of disease from a predominantly *biological* model—an invading pathogen, bio-chemical imbalance, or anatomical abnormality. Similarly, the primary strategy for treatment of disease (physical or mental) in Western medicine has largely been through similar biological means—pharmaceuticals, surgery, chemotherapy, etc. In the past century, Western psychiatry and psychology developed to expand the model of disease pathology and treatment to include *psychological* factors, such as psychotherapy and behavioral modification. Medicine has now embraced these psychological factors of illness and health. Only very recently, really in just the past few decades, have social health and the field of evolutionary psychology affirmed how *social* aspects of human behavior—your environment, upbringing, nurturing, attachment to others, culture, the economy, and even public policy—profoundly affect your health and happiness.

These *biological, psychological,* and *social* dimensions of illness and health promotion are widely accepted today by the medical community. But the missing piece of the healing equation is the *spiritual* aspect of the human condition, evident among the timeless wisdom traditions that continue to flourish today. I'm aware how the concept of spirituality can be elusive or problematic to some. Throughout your Happiness course, spirituality is an overarching term that reflects the universal quest for finding meaning, purpose, and identity in your life—whether via a traditional religion or a personal set of beliefs and practices that connects you to something larger than yourself. This spiritual essence of health and happiness encompasses the myriad array of contemplative practices, rituals, and tools for inner reflection found throughout human culture and history. The spiritual expressions of happiness are equally reflected in your innate capacity to express compassion, empathy, and altruism toward others. Only in the past decade or so have these universal expressions of the human spirit received critical scientific investigation, specifically as they relate to your Happy Brain.

Simply put, there are four Elements for your Happy Brain: biological, psychological, social, and spiritual. It's this emerging Bio-Psycho-Socio-Spiritual model of healthcare that is the revolutionary framework at the heart of *Science of a Happy Brain*. Learning how your brain evolved to engage in these four Elements of the Happy Brain is what differentiates and uniquely situates this book from the deluge of others on the market. By trusting me to be your Happiness professor, I genuinely want you to understand what hundreds of my university students have discovered and what clients from around the world have benefited from—the Bio-Psycho-Socio-Spiritual model is the secret strategy behind *Science of a Happy Brain*. This very strategy helped me on my own healing journey.

Another aim throughout *Science of a Happy Brain* is to help you understand how the convergence between empirical scientific knowledge and experiential spiritual wisdom is a valid mode of revelation. It's this convergent model of science and spirituality that reflects the core philosophy taught throughout my university courses, advanced in ABSRI programs, and embodied in my own life. Don't be surprised to be reading about the neurotransmitter dopamine and the Buddhist concept of *duhkha* in the same lesson. Also, please don't fret if your knowledge of the brain is limited. You can relax in knowing I've done all the heavy work for you. I've made great efforts to explain all the neuroscience research in very accessible and relatable ways that are relevant and applicable into your daily life. The content from your Happiness course will appeal equally to those who appreciate scientific facts and those who embrace spiritual wisdom.

What inspires me most to be your Happiness professor is for you to discover the evolutionary origins of your Happy Brain via the "Social Brain" model of human development. The Social Brain concept of human behavior advances how the human brain formed fundamentally as a social organ to promote survival. Yes, your brain is a social organ. Think of your Social Brain not as a literal part of your brain, like the hippocampus or the neo-cortex, but as a fundamental feature of human behavior and how your brain functions—to be social. In the past decade, there has even been the recent recognition of your "Social Nervous System"—a newly discovered branch of your Autonomic Nervous System that governs your brain's ability to process and regulate your social environment. Learning to exercise your Social Brain is the key to awaken your Happy Brain. In fact, your Social Brain and your Happy Brain are interdependent.

You'll marvel in learning why your Social Brain evolved a strategy to make you experience the social pain from a broken bond as if it were the physical pain from a broken bone. Or how scientists are beginning to understand why cultivating social connection reduces inflammation and accelerates healing in your body, just as effectively as taking aspirin. Most of all, you'll acquire the tools that enable you to apply the latest research about the Social Brain into tangible actions for promoting your Happy Brain.

In my research and in my own personal life, I recognize how happiness is equally an individual pursuit and is one that impacts our world. Your Happiness course concludes with an action plan to harness the science of your Happy Brain to create a more civil culture and stable society. One of the most valued forms of learning comes from hearing other people's stories. It's why I've volunteered for the very first time to share with you my own story with brutal honesty. The courage to be vulnerable and the willingness to be open are the foundation for building trust. My genuine intention to disclose to you one of my deepest personal stories is to earn your faith in allowing me to help you achieve a Happy Brain. I hope learning about how I healed my own pain liberates you from your own suffering and gives you the permission to thrive in life.

I've also personally interviewed and captured real-life events from history and the headlines that exemplify each of the four Elements of your Happy Brain—biological, psychological, social, and spiritual—along with their corresponding four Happiness Strategies. While the names of people whom I've interviewed have been changed for privacy, their stories expressed here are true. Wherever I travel or whomever I encounter on this rich and diverse planet, I know all of you are on the same quest—to experience a life of happiness for yourself and for those you love. Everyone seeks to answer the same question: What does it mean to be a happy human?

But there exists a greater urgency behind writing *Science of a Happy Brain*. It's the Disease of Despair that's dangerously infecting the lives of millions and is one of the greatest health crises of our time. In the past thirty years, I painfully encounter more people enduring depression, PTSD, loneliness, poverty, anxiety, grief, addiction, violence, and hopelessness, all of which fall under this umbrella term. No segment of society is immune to the rampant and rising Disease of Despair. The young and old, rich and poor, gay and straight, liberal and conservative are susceptible. Left unchecked, the Disease of Despair can be fatal and risks affecting future generations.

When it comes to the Disease of Despair, there exist three primary afflictions exponentially on the rise that plague society and sabotage your Happy Brain. They are the afflictions of anger, anxiety, and addiction. Why specifically these three? Anger, anxiety, and addiction don't just hinder your own happiness, they hijack society's happiness. Each of the three afflictions will be explored in greater detail in the context of the Disease of Despair, along with the applied strategies to overcome them in order to achieve your Happy Brain.

The Disease of Despair speaks to a world in crisis and a society desperately seeking hope. It manifests everywhere you look—on the news and in your neighborhoods. It's likely you might have been surprised to learn about the recent "celebrity suicides" that have transpired over the years. I'm sure many of you have certainly battled with despair or desperation in your own life—as I myself did in the years following Mom's suicide. Perhaps you, like I, know the personal pain from having felt helpless seeing someone you love suffering. You may have even come to recognize how the current social narrative of what defines and drives happiness in our world is somehow not working and is in desperate need for re-examining.

If so, this Happiness course is my gift to you. It's my genuine intention for *Science of a Happy Brain* to shed light on the underlying sabotages that negate enduring happiness and the unique strategies that nurture it. View this Happiness course as an antidote to the Disease of Despair manifesting in your life and in the world. There exists a cure to the Disease of Despair, and it resides inside you. It's the strategy you'll learn throughout *Science of a Happy Brain*. The time for this conversation has come. If not now, when?

While the framework behind *Science of a Happy Brain* reflects the university Happiness course that I've been co-teaching over the past seven years, the fundamental concepts and content derive from my own academic research and personal investigations prior to the course. The ten lessons are adapted primarily from the specific lectures that I've delivered in the university Happiness course. They don't include material from those lectures of my friend and colleague, Dr. Gail Stearns, whose value to the course has been indispensable.

I've structured the ten lessons to flow in a specific order. The first five lessons introduce you to the topic of happiness, explain society's Disease of Despair, reveal how happiness evolved in your brain, expose how evolution hijacks your happiness, and outline the power behind your Social Brain. Teaching these lessons to you first is necessary, as they set the stage for you to master the four Happiness Strategies detailed in the remaining lessons in the second half of the Happiness course. Additionally, each lesson includes "Happy Brain Homework" and ends with bonus content available at www. ScienceofaHappyBrain.com for you to engage in and share with others the tools for cultivating your Happy Brain. I want you to benefit from what hundreds of my university students and clients have learned—achieving your Happy Brain is both practical and realistic.

If there's at least one of you out there whose life can be transformed from engaging with *Science of a Happy Brain*, I've accomplished my mission. For every success this book brings in helping someone like you to find happiness and hope, I feel it significantly heals my own pain from not understanding or recognizing Mom's suffering in time. This is why I continue to stay committed. This is why I'm compelled. It's why I care. The opening quote by the Sufi poet Rumi holds special significance in my life. It's the painful wound in my own heart that opened on the day of Mom's suicide that unknowingly allowed the light to illuminate my life and enliven my soul with the love, inspiration, commitment, and wisdom required to be of value to you and benefit to society. By channeling my own suffering into service, I know Mom's suicide didn't happen in vain. This is why I desire to share with you the *Science of a Happy Brain.*

Can a Happy Brain heal the anger, anxiety, and addiction rampant in our society? Does a Happy Brain lead to a life of balance, longevity, and resilience? Do happier people live healthier lives? Is happiness the secret to awaken your purpose and passion in life? Can happy people transform the world into a better place? *Science of a Happy Brain* affirms the answer to all of these questions is a resounding "yes!" Let's get you started on the path to claim your power and benefits of your Happy Brain, a happy life, and becoming a happy human. The world needs you. Happy.

LESSON ONE

THE PURSUIT OF HAPPINESS TAKES PRACTICE

> We hold these truths to be self-evident, that
> all men are created equal, that they are endowed
> by their Creator with certain unalienable Rights,
> that among these are Life, Liberty and the pursuit
> of Happiness.
>
> —United States Declaration of Independence

Your Right to Happiness

Welcome to your Happiness course. I'm genuinely glad you get to be part of this valuable class. It probably comes as no surprise, I absolutely love teaching it, just as much as I know you'll enjoy taking it. Even though it's been seven years since I began annually teaching the Happiness course, I remain just as enthusiastic today imparting to you the latest strategies for you to build your Happy Brain.

My intention for offering to you this Happiness course is attributed to one obvious reason—everyone wants to know the secrets for experiencing happiness. The desire for a happy life transcends age, race, religion, culture, gender, sexuality, class, politics, and history. Even the Founding Fathers of the United States famously proclaimed when drafting the Declaration of Independence, everyone is endowed with the unalienable Rights of "Life, Liberty and the pursuit of

Happiness." The framers of the American Constitution believed that like life and liberty, the pursuit of happiness is your universal right. But there's one problem.

Reflecting as your Happiness professor and from my own personal journey, I've come to realize that desiring happiness, pursuing happiness, and achieving happiness are very different aspirations. As a fond student of history, I'm keenly aware Thomas Jefferson—who originally drafted the Declaration of Independence—wasn't a perfect human being. Despite how modern society judges him, you can still admire his visionary words and wisdom. While Jefferson declared that you're all endowed with the right to happiness, there's one serious disclaimer inherent in this famous document. Let's be realistic; while you may desire happiness, attaining happiness is no guarantee.

Notice how Thomas Jefferson didn't just write "Life, Liberty and Happiness." He specifically penned that it's "Life, Liberty and the *pursuit of Happiness*." Even back in 1776, Jefferson knew happiness isn't a guarantee in life. You have to pursue happiness; it doesn't naturally come to you. Well, guess what? It's exactly what timeless spiritual wisdom and current brain science research affirm—your right to happiness isn't assured. Way to go, Tom! You just got an A+ in the Happiness course.

While Jefferson declared happiness to be a human right—albeit tragically not a right for everyone in his time—he knew very well the notion of happiness is something you have to pursue in life. The Founding Fathers realized it's the *pursuit of Happiness* that is the fundamental right you're entitled to—not happiness itself. Just because you pursue something, doesn't mean you'll always get it, right?

Here's your first important point to learn in your Happiness course: *The pursuit of happiness is more than a promise; the pursuit of happiness is a practice.*

It's the very reason for creating the Happiness course and the aim of the next ten lessons—to teach you the skills requisite to pursue and practice happiness. Like with any other of your goals in life—whether losing weight, getting into a top college, investing for retirement, competing in a marathon, or achieving a dream career—

happiness is something you have to work for and pursue with practice and perseverance. I now extend to you the same valuable insights established in this Happiness course for you to create your own strategy in the pursuit of happiness. The lessons outlined reveal how to manifest a life of happiness. It begins by learning to cultivate your Happy Brain. This is what you're about to discover and I plan to share with you. The science of a Happy Brain requires practice. Let's start with your first lesson and exercise for the class.

I invite you to engage in your first task, which for many of you probably will be the most thought-provoking one in your Happiness course. The assignment is for you to answer a simple question: What is happiness? To facilitate this task, I want you to write a "happiness letter" in the form of a personal letter to yourself. You have the option to write your "happiness letter" by hand. If you prefer to complete this assignment on your computer or confidentially online, please go to www.ScienceofaHappyBrain.com where you'll be instructed how to compose your personal letter. You can rest assured knowing that your online letter will remain private and only available to you. Whichever method you choose, please write detailed reflections for the following questions:

1) Why is achieving happiness important to me?
2) What currently brings me happiness in my life?
3) What thoughts, actions, behaviors, or circumstances presently undermine happiness in my life?
4) Is there a specific issue in my life at the moment that diminishes my happiness?
5) What does an ideal life of happiness look like to me?

Again, it's important you take your time in thoughtfully answering these five relevant questions before moving on with the first lesson.

If you composed a handwritten letter, please enclose it in a sealed envelope and keep it in a secure place where you'll remember. You're even welcome to place the envelope in the pages toward the end of the book, as you'll be opening your "happiness letter" once you get to Lesson Ten. If you opted to write your letter online, you'll be instructed how to save and retrieve it for later.

Why am I asking you to engage in this introductory task? First, it gets you right away to start thinking about what exactly happiness is and what it means to you. Second, I want you to determine if and how your personal idea of happiness changes toward the end of your Happiness course. The other intention behind this task is to help you become more aware of the challenges posed when trying to define what exactly is happiness. While many of you likely know what happiness *is not*, unfortunately, no one ever tells you what exactly happiness is. So again, I pose the question "What is happiness?" Are you ready to find out? If so, let's continue with the first lesson in your Happiness course.

What Is Happiness?

Defining happiness is a tough task. Answering this question is the path I've embarked upon over the past two decades. The question of what defines happiness is one I've personally struggled with that found me desperately seeking answers in the halls of academia and in holy ashrams. The wisdom gained over the years has revealed insights and truths I now wish to share with you.

Very few people reach adulthood knowing what cultivates genuine happiness, where it resides, and how to sustain it. You all may desire happiness, yet so many don't really even know what it is. In order to help you better recognize what happiness is, it's helpful to reframe how society traditionally has come to view happiness. Here's an example of how that looks.

For a very long time, the fields of medicine and psychiatry have focused on treating what's wrong with you. Only recently have the emerging fields of holistic health and positive psychology become concerned on what's right with you—what makes you healthy and happy. What makes you not just survive; what makes you thrive. Most people only know happiness as the absence of stress and suffering. It's why being able to define "happiness" by what it is—versus by what it's not—can be quite a challenge for many of you seeking happiness in life. It's rather likely that you've simply never been taught how to frame happiness in the positive by what it exactly is. Just as you probably recognize health is much more than the elimination of illness, you need to view happiness as much more than a life free from hardship. For example, I personally know people who enjoy comfortable and prosperous lives who experience misery. Likewise, I've met people who endure severe hardship, yet are amazingly content with life.

I don't believe there's such a thing as a "perfect life," nor do I believe in the existence of utopia. Pain, hardship, despair, and struggle are embedded into the human equation. As you'll soon discover, they actually have to be. I think you can glean from your own experiences how the meaning of life would be empty without moments of strife and struggle, just as I came to realize how Mom's suicide became that defining moment for me. This is the very reason why your first task in the Happiness course is to write your happiness letter—to get you thinking about what exactly constitutes your happiness and what defines a happy life. It's why you need a strategy that actively promotes happiness versus one that only eliminates stress and suffering.

Over the next ten lessons you'll discover this strategy for happiness is the Bio-Psycho-Socio-Spiritual model that draws from both current research in brain science and timeless spiritual traditions. Throughout your Happiness course you'll learn how the four Elements of Happiness—biological, psychological, social, and spiritual—relate to the four corresponding Happiness Strategies for your Happy Brain. Let me introduce to you how the four Happiness Strategies align with the Bio-Psycho-Socio-Spiritual model by revealing the 4 Cs of your Happy Brain: *Comfort*, *Contribution*, *Connection*, and *Compassion*. Here's how this model looks:

1) The *Biological* Element of Happiness derives from the Happiness Strategy of *Comfort*.
2) The *Psychological* Element of Happiness occurs from experiencing the Happiness Strategy of *Contribution*.

3) The *Social* Element of Happiness is associated with the Happiness Strategy of *Connection*.

4) The *Spiritual* Element of Happiness manifests through the Happiness Strategy of *Compassion*.

Now that you've been exposed to an overview of the four Happiness Strategies, let's explore why the desire for happiness remains such a struggle in today's world. Specifically, what are you doing to sabotage happiness? What are the consequences for you and for society when you lack the benefits from achieving a Happy Brain?

The Disease of Despair

Now that you've written in your happiness letter what happiness means to you personally, let's explore how happiness relates to society. Specifically, are there any major global issues, social crises, or health factors society faces that diminish or hijack happiness? I bet you can. Here are some that you might agree are pressing issues in today's world: Depression, stress, anxiety, poverty, food scarcity, the environment, poor diet, homelessness, sexual abuse, addiction, PTSD, no exercise, hooked on technology, social media status, consumerism, war, hopelessness, terrorism, political division, crime, greed, social isolation, racism, gun violence, income inequality, economic injustice, loneliness, drive to succeed, and peer pressure are several factors. There are likely more.

I think you'd agree that all of these issues in some way do currently contribute to society's Happiness Crisis. But it's much worse, I'm afraid. What's witnessed today is more than a Happiness Crisis—it's morphed into a dangerous epidemic.

There's an unrecognized and pervasive disease affecting society today. It's not a virus, it's not the flu, but it's just as contagious and deadly. In the past few decades, this disease has proliferated to cause the premature deaths of millions. Chances are you know someone who currently suffers from or has succumbed to this illness. Maybe you've witnessed firsthand this disease silently spreading in your families, neighborhoods, schools, and workplaces. No vaccine, no pill can completely immunize you from this disease. Any idea what this deadly epidemic is? It's society's Disease of Despair.

When you hear or read this term "Disease of Despair," what comes to your mind? Well, whether it's addiction, suicide, PTSD, loneliness, alcohol abuse, drug overdose, societal discord, a general feeling of hopelessness, or even many of the issues previously mentioned, they reveal and are expressions of this Disease of Despair. To be clear, the Disease of Despair reflects more than just a temporary feeling of sadness or grief you experience in life at some point. The Disease of Despair refers to the health crisis and the growing death rate—along with the social and economic toll it bears—that this epidemic plays out in today's world when living in an age of chronic anger, anxiety, and addiction. Here's why the afflictions of anger, anxiety, and addiction amplify society's Disease of Despair.

Anger can rightfully result when someone cuts you off while driving on the highway or when you learn your partner is cheating on you. The anger in the context of the Disease of Despair is the growing rage and widespread contempt witnessed in our politics, society, and media on a daily basis. While anger can certainly be a healthy emotion to help you process feelings of being wronged, the collective anger prevalent today stems from injustice, discontentment, malice, hate, intolerance, and fear. When this form of violent anger runs amok in your life and in society, it sabotages your Happy Brain and spreads the Disease of Despair.

The most common psychological disorder that hijacks the health and happiness of most Americans is anxiety. As a university professor, I witness this affliction directly. It's truly disturbing to know how more incoming students struggle with anxiety and the ability to cope with the rigorous demands of college and life. Anxiety can result from a variety of factors—economic uncertainty, health issues, poverty, unemployment due to automation, political strife, and peer pressure are just a few issues manifesting today. It should also be clear that stress isn't the same as anxiety. While everyone experiences stress on a regular basis, stress tends to be the product of your reaction to external situations in the moment. Anxiety, on the other hand, is an internal response to stress beyond the present moment. From the perspective of brain science and evolutionary psychology, stress is the way you react to temporary threats in your life. Anxiety is more chronic that results when the feeling of panic endures, even after the momentary stress subsides. The affliction of anxiety is another expression of society's greater Disease of Despair.

Addiction manifests beyond substance abuse. The rise in addiction to consumerism, technology, online gaming, and social media also advances angst and anguish throughout the world. In whichever form addiction occurs, you surely know how it disrupts a person's well-being and strains society. While the cause of and cure for addiction are being actively researched, society still experiences the tragic rise in depression and deaths attributed to addiction. It's why I've chosen to include addiction as a dangerous affliction behind society's Disease of Despair. As you'll discover in subsequent lessons, the impact that anger, anxiety, and addiction pose on society is interconnected and appears to be the result from a complex array of social, cultural, economic, and personal factors that disrupt primal systems in your brain. Unchecked, the three afflictions of anger, anxiety, and addiction collectively undermine your Happy Brain.

So how strongly is the Disease of Despair affecting people today? You already know my own story and personal investment around this issue. Mom is someone I believe was a victim to the Disease of Despair. I'd even define myself gripped with ongoing depression and anxiety in the years after Mom's suicide as being someone affected by this epidemic. As a survivor of a family member's suicide, I'm keenly sensitive to the pain and emotional scar it leaves for those of you who've lost loved ones. It's why I'm devastated whenever I read or hear stories about people who've died from or acted on thoughts of suicide. While Mom's suicide remains traumatic for me, what continues to sadden me is how the Disease of Despair unnecessarily continues to take the lives of those you love.

It wasn't just Mom's suicide decades ago that led me on the path to become a leading voice and researcher in the science of happiness today. Another fairly recent and significant event transpired that alerted me to the severity the Disease of Despair inflicts upon society.

As an academic, I endeavor to stay on top of current research and findings coming from the fields of brain science and behavioral health. Little did I know how a critical report would become another catalyst to change my life's direction and reframe my life's purpose.

It was the day before I was set to give a keynote speech here in Southern California on "Resilience, Healing, and the Brain" for Orange County's Mental Health Care Agency. The CEO of ABSRI, Paul, forwarded to me an article from the April 2016 issue of *The Economist* he thought would be relevant for my presentation. This one article sparked my curiosity to investigate the cause behind the Disease of Despair. The information contained in the article Paul sent to me was so pertinent, I actually had to revise my presentation the night before I was set to give for the hundred or so psychologists, social workers, and mental health providers the next morning.

Furthermore, there was one particular statistic from this article that was so pivotal it's important I share it with you in this opening lesson.

Figure 1

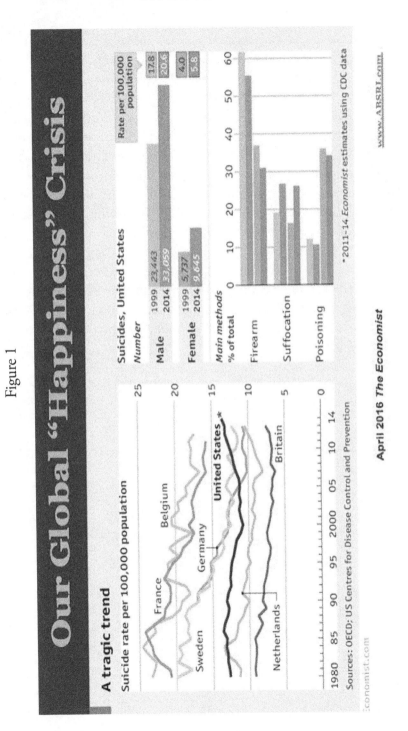

Why is this graph such a powerful wake-up call that I felt the need to share it with you in this lesson of your Happiness course? This study compiled by the US Centers for Disease Control and Prevention reveals a shocking statistic. Factoring in for age-adjustment, *The Economist* article states, "The suicide rate in the US rose 24% from 1999 to 2014 and is approaching a 30-year high."[1]

Naming or identifying this Disease of Despair may sound alarmist, but more statistics and facts back up this assertion. Here's another revealing study how severe this epidemic has become for society. From 1999 to 2015, deaths related to alcohol abuse, from suicide, or drug overdose in the United States rose from 23.1 to 39.7 per 100,000 people.[2] In case you're wondering, that's a spike of 72 percent. You don't have to be a researcher or academic to know something is going terribly wrong. The Disease of Despair is rampant, and the situation appears to be getting worse. I'm convinced that if not properly addressed, the Disease of Despair is positioned to be the next big crisis of the current and future generations, not to mention the burden it will have on our economy, society, and health-care system.

What's exactly attributing to the spike in US suicide? Why do we see a precipitous increase in the Disease of Despair? These are the questions I've been vigorously investigating over the past couple of years since reading that decisive article in May 2016. Unfortunately, there's no one simple answer. The reasons behind the rise in the Disease of Despair are notably intertwined and complex. But there appears to be one culprit: the increasing decline of social support systems and social resilience in the United States over the past few decades. Of course, this isn't the only factor accounting for the Disease of Despair, but keep in mind this one facet as you move into future lessons. Just as the science of a Happy Brain will be explored through the Bio-Psycho-Socio-Spiritual model, there equally exist biological, psychological, social, and spiritual dimensions that fuel our nation's Disease of Despair.

[1.] "American suicides return to a disturbing 30-year high," *The Economist*, Apr. 28, 2016.

[2.] Sarah Toy and Jayne O'Donnell, "Deaths from drugs, alcohol and suicide could hit 1.6M over the next decade, report says," *USA Today*, Nov. 21, 2017.

If you're curious why I chose balance, longevity, and resilience as the three outcomes of your Happy Brain, it's due to the Disease of Despair and its detrimental impact on society. Lacking the tools for achieving your Happy Brain leaves you susceptible to chaos, prone to illness, and exposed to vulnerability in the face of adversity and stress. What you'll learn in future lessons is how your Happy Brain creates balance, longevity, and resilience in life and counters the rampant levels of anger, anxiety, and addiction that trigger the Disease of Despair.

The main point I want to make is how society is in the midst of an epidemic that is taking more lives than necessary. One aim for your Happiness course is more than just to provide you with the tools for achieving personal happiness; its focus is to advance how as a society we can prevent the spread of the Disease of Despair from taking more lives. A cure exists. It's the primary theme you'll learn in the lessons over the Happiness course. Why's this so important? If there's one of you whose life I can spare from succumbing to the Disease of Despair, I've successfully accomplished my role as your Happiness professor. That's why I offer the Happiness course—to advance a shared strategy for promoting both individual and societal happiness. My motto for the course and for my life's mission continues to be: *Happy brains make happy people. Happy people make a happy world.*

Let's explore the strategy for making that possible by examining the origin of human happiness in the context of evolution and how nature wired your brain to hijack your happiness. You're ready for Lesson Two.

Bonus Content

Visit www.ScienceofaHappyBrain.com to engage in the following activities:
- Invite others you know to write their own happiness letter.
- Enjoy free content related to this lesson on how to control anger, anxiety, and addiction that sabotage your Happy Brain.
- To learn more about how you can help donate or help prevent suicide, please visit https://afsp.org/

LESSON TWO

YOUR BRAIN EVOLVED FOR SURVIVAL, NOT HAPPINESS

> Anyone can be happy by simply training their brain.
>
> —Matthieu Ricard

Stress and Your Stone-Age Tribe Brain

It's safe to say there are few things in life that I despise more than the torment of having to drive during the height of rush hour on the freeways where I live in Southern California—especially on a very hot day. It's a form of misery I greatly try to avoid, but a situation I inevitably found myself in one late summer evening in 2012 driving the fifty miles from Orange County to the secluded home I was living in at the time located in the remote canyons near Pacific Palisades. After crawling up the 405 Freeway for over ninety minutes in ninety-degree heat at 6pm, I could feel my stress mounting and the tension increasing in my muscles with every minute stuck behind the steering wheel.

Pulling into the driveway of the home and being surrounded by the soothing sights of nature, I was finally able to exhale and release all the stress and tension experienced from the taxing commute. That is, until I opened the door of the car and nearly stepped on a three-foot long rattlesnake basking on the driveway mere inches from my left leg. To make it worse, the rattlesnake was coiled facing me and making aggressive sounds with its tail. Without even having to think, my brain instinctively went into auto-pilot. I jumped back into the safety of my car and slammed the door shut just in time before it could strike. After honking the horn for a few seconds and relocating the car, I saw the rattlesnake slither back into the wild bush of the mountainside.

After a few minutes of calming myself down with some more deep breaths, I managed to gain my composure, exit the car, and enter the house. For the rest of the evening, there was only one thing preoccupying my thoughts—not the stress from a rattling drive, but the anxiety from a close rattlesnake bite. I recount this story as a way to introduce to you the biological function of human stress and how stress simultaneously sabotages and supports your Happy Brain.

Studying the function of stress and the nature of human suffering is an integral component in your Happiness course, which is why I need to share it with you in this lesson. What is stress? Why does your brain produce it? What causes suffering in life? How do stress and suffering sabotage your Happy Brain? Most importantly, what can you do to change it? While these have been timeless questions pondered and deliberated upon by philosophers, theologians, and spiritual teachers, there now exists a novel lens through which the origin of stress and the nature of suffering can be explored—brain science.

Brace yourself for what I'm about to say. Your brain didn't evolve for happiness. Nature doesn't care about your happiness; it only cares about your survival. It's the reason why evolution primed your brain to experience stress.

I know, that one may come as a shock, and I'm sorry to be the bearer of bad news, folks. But, it's true—your brain evolved to make it nearly impossible for you to eliminate stress from your life. Like death and taxes, stress and suffering are inevitable aspects of life and are intimately linked. No matter how hard you try, you can never eradicate stress entirely. To be more precise, evolution made it virtually impossible to excise the stress-response system from your brain.

Despite your external differences in religion, language, race, gender, sexuality, politics, and class, you all are unified by the shared internal mechanisms and functional biology of your human brain. Just as the quest for happiness is universal, so too is the basic functional anatomy of your brain. While human behavior can vary, the underlying structure of the brain's stress-response system is shared among all humans.

It's why I've come to view the brain as a neutral terrain to explore what makes you tick and how you all can apply brain science for achieving your Happy Brain and a life of balance, longevity, and resilience. This is the primary reason and unique strategy why I choose to explore the concept of happiness through the lens of brain science and human behavior. It's also why you have the potential to achieve a Happy Brain. Let's explore why your brain evolved to create stress, how stress relates to an important term called your "Stone-Age Tribe brain" and how they both sabotage your ability to benefit from a Happy Brain.

The main point for you in this lesson—in the context of evolutionary biology and developmental psychology—is to understand how your brain equates survival with happiness. If you're ready, here's an experiential exercise I want you to try that will help you better to grasp why this is true. To do so, let's take a trip into the past—the way distant past of your ancient ancestors and peer into your "Stone-Age Tribe brain."

After you've finished this paragraph, I want you to imagine yourself as one of your ancient human ancestors going back in time to 10,000 BCE to the Stone Age. You're all alone in the desolate, open plains of ancient Earth. You're naked, cold, hungry, tired, and thirsty. You've obviously got no cell phone, matches, flashlight, or GPS system to help you out. To make it worse, night is rapidly approaching, and the terrifying sounds of hungry predators are growing louder. Now if possible, for the next ten seconds I want you to close your eyes and put yourself in this imaginary situation and feel what it's like being in this very vulnerable state—alone, cold, hungry, exhausted, and terrified.

What were you just feeling in your body? Did you experience any anxiety, fear, panic, or dread? Maybe your heart was racing or perhaps you noticed your gut tighten. If you were feeling any sense of discomfort from this hypothetical situation, you're not alone.

If you felt any uneasiness or panic in your body, you know exactly how your distant ancestors felt on a constant basis. Life in the Stone Age wasn't the proverbial "walk in the park," by any means. Ancient humans lived in a perpetual state of vulnerability and unpredictability. Contrary to what you might think, the human brain didn't emerge into its present form all at once. It evolved gradually in specific stages and layers over the course of hundreds of thousands of years.

One primal function of your brain—relevant for this lesson on stress and how it sabotages your happiness—is your Stone-Age Tribe brain. So how does stress relate to your Stone-Age Tribe brain? The discomfort you likely were feeling from this last exercise is precisely what your Stone-Age Tribe brain evolved to do—for you to experience stress by alerting you to dangers in your environment that threaten your life. The primary function of your Stone-Age Tribe brain is to promote survival. Due to evolution's strategy for your Stone-Age Tribe brain to react instinctively to threats in your environment, it's the reason why stress is so deeply part of the human condition. Stress and your Stone-Age Tribe brain go hand in hand, folks.

Just for clarity, the Stone-Age Tribe brain isn't a scientific term. You won't find it used in research journals or even by other academics. In fact, it's not even a specific region or layer of your brain. If you're familiar with your brain's "fight-flight-freeze response" or know about the brain's amygdala that triggers your "stress response" system, your Stone-Age Tribe brain encompasses both of them. Additionally, there exist other systems and regions of your brain that relate to your Stone-Age Tribe brain that I'll save for future lessons. For now, just know that the Stone-Age Tribe brain is the lay-person's term I've been using in the Happiness course and my training seminars for the past few years, which rightfully describes the function of stress and how it hijacks your Happy Brain. For now, just focus on the "Stone-Age" aspect of the term Stone-Age Tribe brain and leave the

"Tribe" component for later. How exactly does your Stone-Age Tribe brain relate to your Happy Brain?

How I see it, there are essentially three primary drives sought out by your Stone-Age Tribe brain—safety, security, and stability. Survival was the primary purpose of life for your Stone-Age ancestors. Your Stone-Age Tribe brain just wants you to live another day. Nothing else matters. It's exactly the reason why you likely felt uneasiness in your body just a few minutes ago imagining how brutal life was back in the Stone Age. If you were literally in that situation, it would've been a clear survival threat for you. Here's what you need to know from this lesson—both the origin and sabotage of your happiness reside in your Stone-Age Tribe brain. Why? Your Stone-Age Tribe brain associates happiness with survival. Your Stone-Age Tribe brain equates happiness as seeking safety, security, and stability.

Yet, survival meant more than your getting to live another day; it also meant your chances for having sex would increase. Yup, sex! Survival meant humans would reproduce offspring, thus, ensuring the continuity of the human species. As is known from evolutionary biology, any anatomical or biological trait that serves as a strategy for survival of the species gets passed down into the genes of the offspring. Your Stone-Age Tribe brain's stress-response system is that clever tactic for survival. This is the simple rationale for how and why stress continues to be a vital aspect of the human condition. Stress got you to survive, which got you to reproduce, which got more humans on the planet. Nature loves this. Nature wants you to experience stress to increase your odds for survival. In a weird and perverse way, stress gets you to survive. Since survival equates to happiness, stress and happiness become interrelated in your Stone-Age Tribe brain. Make sense?

Your Stone-Age Tribe brain became nature's cunning strategy to alert you when threats to your survival are imminent and present. It doesn't matter whether those threats used to manifest as an approaching enemy armed with a deadly club or currently exist today as the anxiety over not being able to pay your rent or mortgage. In each of these scenarios, your Stone-Age Tribe brain is operating on red alert and equally generates stress in your brain, body, and being.

Thanks to stress and the Stone-Age Tribe brain, humanity survived. But it comes at a very steep price.

Most of you would agree it would be foolish—not to mention outright impossible—opting to get rid of your body's respiratory or circulatory system. Science shows how both of these systems are essential for life. Similarly, your Stone-Age Tribe brain contains a built-in stress-response system that regulates your survival. In fact, all the various systems contained in your body evolved over the course of thousand of years and have been fine-tuned for one goal—survival of the species. Just as your breath and blood are essential for life, similarly stress serves a crucial component for human survival.

This relationship between stress and happiness is a core feature explored in my first book *Brain, Body & Being*, in which I share, "The moment [stress] kicks in, the *brain* immediately alerts your *body*. Stress hormones cortisol and adrenaline are unleashed in your bloodstream. This flood of stress chemicals triggered by the brain into the body has a significant impact on your overall emotional, psychological, and mental state of *being*."[3] Stress and suffering span your brain, body, and being. If stress is a biological feature of the human condition, the emotional and psychological counterpart to stress is suffering. You'll actually discover the suffering aspect of the Stone-Age Tribe brain in the next lesson. For now, let's stick to how stress sabotages your Happy Brain.

You don't have to be a scientist to realize that for your ancient ancestors, life was undoubtedly harsh. Foraging for food was treacherous. Safe and warm shelters were hard to find. Death lurked everywhere. Unrelenting hardship was a fact of life. Just getting to live another day was a cause for great rejoicing. Anything in the environment that jeopardized the ability for making it just one more day became a source of stress. Threatening predators, competing foes, starvation, lack of sleep, and exposure to the elements were major stressors for early humans—and sadly still for many people today. As

---

3. Jay Kumar, *Brain, Body & Being: Five Secrets for Achieving Authentic Health & Happiness* (Price International Publishers, 2014), 9.

much as you likely try to avoid or minimize stress in your life, nature simply has another plan. Let's find out exactly what that strategy is.

Nature's Gamble on Happiness

As someone who delights in discovering the link between brain science and human behavior, the most amazing aspect about your brain's stress-response system is how it gets equally triggered whether the threat to your survival is presently occurring or was remembered from your past. Even if the threat is real or perceived, your Stone-Age Tribe brain reacts in precisely the same way—you experience stress.

The Stone-Age Tribe brain lurks and is fully operational within everyone—even today. As much as you all still rely upon your Stone-Age Tribe brain for survival, it's also the culprit that hijacks your happiness. Why? Your Stone-Age Tribe brain is incapable of differentiating whether threats in your environment are real or perceived. Here's a great example to understand why that is.

Your ancient ancestors wandered around the unrelenting harsh terrains of Earth trying to survive. In any given moment, there were two options constantly available to them. Option 1: Thinking there was a lion in the bush even when there wasn't one. Option 2: Thinking there was no lion in the bush even when there was one. The first option simply created constant anxiety; the second option ensured death. So which option would you choose? Which option favors survival? The first one, obviously. This example also helps to better frame the evolutionary rationale around why so many people are prone to anxiety. While no one voluntarily opts to live in a state of unrelenting stress and anxiety, your Stone-Age Tribe brain is deliberately wired in such a way as a strategy for survival of the species.

Here's another valuable point from this lesson. Your Stone-Age Tribe brain evolved for safety, security, and stability. But to achieve those goals, your Stone-Age Tribe brain intentionally provokes you to exist in a constant state of strife, scarcity, and suspicion. As much as stress is a functional tactic for survival, the trade-off occurs as your Stone-Age Tribe brain's ability to trick you into experiencing unnecessary anxiety. Isn't that just wonderful?

Why on Earth would your Stone-Age Tribe Brain do this to you? It did so to enhance your odds for survival. The alternative was death. Mother Nature isn't always kind, but Mother Nature is exceptionally clever. She took a gamble and placed the bet on the stress-response system and won. Having your Stone-Age Tribe brain operate in a constant state of low-grade anxiety—under strife, scarcity, and suspicion—was worth the risk. Nature's gamble paid off, and from taking that risk, the human species is still going strong.

Putting aside for the moment all aspects of spirituality, philosophy, or morality, from the perspective of evolution, there exists one primal goal for human existence—survival. Whether it was thousands of years ago or today, your brain's stress-response system still alerts you to when there is a looming threat or potential danger jeopardizing your safety, security, and stability. Do you now see how stress got to be such an important aspect of human survival?

To the best of our knowledge, humans are the sole species that can get stressed out over a situation that hasn't even yet occurred or go into panic over a situation that isn't a legitimate threat to your life. We know it best as anxiety. To help illuminate the distinction between stress and anxiety, let's return to the story of my driving during rush-hour traffic and nearly being bitten by the rattlesnake. Although there was no clear nor imminent danger to my life while driving on the freeway, I was experiencing prolonged, low-grade anxiety from anticipating how long it would take for me to drive home during rush-hour. Compare that non-threatening situation to the high-level of instantaneous stress produced from the real peril to my health from the rattlesnake I almost stepped on upon exiting my car. In both instances, my stress-response system was operating at various degrees of activity that produced the similar biological reactions of an accelerated heart-rate, shallow breath, and tensing of my body. As many of you can likely attest, the level of anxiety felt from anticipating a final exam or a major presentation you have to give in front of hundreds of strangers—neither a real nor present threat to your life—can elicit the same biological reactions for panic as nearly stepping on an angry rattlesnake.

Here's one big take-away from your Happiness course I want you to remember—whether you're trying to avoid a head-on collision on the highway (a real threat to your life), running to catch your departing flight at the airport (a perceived threat), or losing sleep over that meeting with your overbearing boss in the morning (a potential threat), your Stone-Age Tribe brain evolved to process these situations in the exact same way. In each of these scenarios your Stone-Age Tribe brain produces stress in the moment to react to an imminent threat and generates anxiety in anticipation over a potential threat yet to occur. The gist from today's lesson is this. Your Stone-Age Tribe brain developed for one primary function—*to remember stressful situations from your past, react to dangers in your present, and anticipate perceived threats in your future.*

Through the lens of evolutionary biology, nature's gamble continues to be one incredibly amazing feat for humans, as it became a powerful advantage for survival. Hard to imagine, but your Stone-Age Tribe brain is your best ally in life. Without it and the brain's accompanying stress-response system, humans would've become extinct a long time ago. Your Stone-Age Tribe brain is a good thing, right?

Well, sort of. As you'll find out in future lessons, despite the evolutionary advantage of your Stone-Age Tribe brain to promote survival, there's a dark aspect to it. If you recall, your Stone-Age Tribe brain's default mode is strife, scarcity, and suspicion. As a result, it has the potential for people individually and collectively to react with aggression, rage, and intolerance toward others whenever you perceive a survival threat. As much as you need your Stone-Age Tribe brain, when left unchecked it can lead to harmful behaviors such as greed, violence, bigotry, apathy, distrust, and fear of the other. War, racism, authoritarianism, social injustice, tribalism, genocide, and political discord are all negative products of your Stone-Age Tribe brain manifesting on the societal level. Even PTSD, addiction, and anxiety-disorders are behavioral outcomes that originate in your Stone-Age Tribe brain.

For now, here's another point relevant for your goal to a Happy Brain. Fortunately, even though many of you no longer have to be preoccupied with the hardships your Stone-Age ancestors endured on a constant basis, sadly, the vast majority of people today still react to life's situations via the primal Stone-Age Tribe brain every single hour of the day. Going about your day constantly operating out of your Stone-Age Tribe brain's state of strife, scarcity, and suspicion is one major factor that hijacks happiness and fuels society's Disease of Despair witnessed as the three great afflictions of anger, anxiety, and addiction. The more you learn not to become a prisoner to your Stone-Age Tribe brain, the more balance, longevity, and resilience you'll manifest in life.

It's truly a double-edged sword. Stress—the very functional strategy that evolved for your survival—is what also sabotages your Happy Brain, your ability to achieve happiness in life, and society's quest for peace and prosperity. The following table summarizes these points.

Table 1

STRESS	ANXIETY
Your Stone-Age Tribe brain creates momentary stress when present situations threaten your:	Your Stone-Age Tribe brain creates chronic anxiety when you anticipate:
Safety	Strife
Security	Scarcity
Stability	Suspicion

Focus on the Bad, Forget the Good

Here's the final and important point from this lesson for you to know that explains why achieving your Happy Brain requires tremendous effort. Your Stone-Age Tribe brain evolved to focus on the bad and forget the good. It's a concept sometimes referred to as your brain's *negativity bias.* The Stone-Age Tribe brain evolved to focus on negative experiences and register stressful situations more strongly than remembering positive ones. Here's how I want you to understand it.

I've often heard your brain's negativity bias as best explained by the following phrase: "Your brain is like Velcro for negative experiences and like Teflon for positive ones."[4] What that means is your Stone-Age Tribe brain excels at making the bad experiences stick, while making the good ones slip away. This concept is the essence behind your brain's negativity bias—your brain is biased to remember more effectively the stressful and negative experiences than the joyful, happy ones. Why? Let's discover it with another exercise for you to grasp how your brain's negativity bias operates.

You wake up Monday morning to find out your best friend, who lives across the country and that you haven't seen in years, is going to be in town next weekend. You go to the kitchen and are surprised your roommate or partner has already made coffee and breakfast for you both. You drive to work and immediately find the perfect parking spot. You get a text from your kid in college saying he got an A+ on his research paper in Dr. Jay's Happiness course. Your boss invites you into her office to tell you that you're getting a promotion and a pay raise. Your day just keeps getting better and better. Even the weather is gorgeous. It's such a beautiful evening, before driving home from work you decide to treat yourself to your favorite flavor of ice cream. You're riding high with joy and think nothing can bring you down.

Your Happy Brain is in high mode—that is, until you return to your car after relishing your ice cream and are stunned to see the window to your car smashed and items stolen from inside. Your Happy Brain just burst like a poked balloon. After hours speaking with the police, calling a tow truck, getting a rental car, and dealing with your insurance company, you finally drive back home, sulking the entire way over your poor luck. Even though you had a series of amazing events happen in the course of your day, the most recent negative situation is predominating your thoughts—the fact that your car got broken into earlier. That, my friends, is your brain's

---

4. Rick Hanson, "Taking in the Good," www.psychology.com, July 6, 2010.

negativity bias in a nutshell. As I said earlier: Your brain is like Velcro for negative experiences and like Teflon for positive ones. The stress you felt from dealing with the mishap and the new anxiety faced over the time and money required to fix the damage to your car sticks like Velcro in your mind. The string of fortunate events in your day that brought you happiness simply slide away like Teflon.

Why I enjoy doing this exercise is that it nicely explains how your brain's negativity bias sabotages your happiness. Specifically, I hope it helps you understand why stress and anxiety, more so than calm and contentment, are more strongly experienced in your daily life. Your brain's negativity bias is directly related to your Stone-Age Tribe brain's natural default setting for strife, scarcity, and suspicion. If you recall, it was more advantageous for your ancient ancestors to remember the stress accompanied from being chased by a lion or nearly dying from eating a poisonous fruit—in order to avoid repeating those situations—than the joy felt from watching a sunset or playing with your kids. Your Stone-Age Tribe brain's negativity bias—focusing on the bad while forgetting the good—is another reason why you actively have to work for and pursue happiness in life. Why? Nature doesn't care about your Happy Brain; it cares about your survival.

Evolution is ruthlessly efficient, as it has only one goal in mind—survival of the species. It's why opposable thumbs for grasping tools, vocal cords for speech, and the bones and muscles for walking upright continue to be part of human biology. Similarly, the negativity bias—which relates directly to your Stone-Age Tribe brain and to the stress-response system—remains a strategic behavioral trait that enhances survival. If they didn't, none of these human attributes would have developed. Nature deplores inefficiency. Inefficiency results in extinction.

Your Stone-Age Tribe brain naturally favors stress over happiness; it prefers anxiety over equanimity. It's exactly how nature wants it to be. You'll explore the precise neural mechanisms behind the stress-response system and how it sabotages your Happy Brain later. For now, my goal in this lesson is to introduce to you the basic function of how stress became an evolutionary strategy for your survival and why experiencing unnecessary anxiety became a crucial tactic for the human species.

The basic point I want you to remember is how anything in your environment that triggers your brain's ability for you to experience stress got wired into your memory. Being able to recall and to anticipate these remembered stressors in life—experienced as anxiety—became advantageous for human survival. For your Stone-Age Tribe brain survival equates with happiness.

You're probably thinking: *Is this nature's perverse idea of a cruel joke?* That's right, it is. Stress and anxiety evolved as fundamental features of your brain to promote survival. To be blunt, nature "doesn't give a damn" about your Happy Brain; nature only cares about your survival and continuity of the species. While the rise in anxiety levels—one tangible manifestation of the Disease of Despair—is a real issue, many are left unaware how you have the innate ability to manage stress and anxiety in your life. You've got to learn how to outsmart nature and evolution if you want a Happy Brain. It's the reason why achieving your Happy Brain takes perseverance and practice.

Before exploring the powerful strategy for achieving your Happy Brain, you need to be aware of one more primal tactic nature had in store for ensuring survival. Hands down, it's even more cruel than the way your brain's stress-response system and negativity bias thwart your happiness. It's also another culprit behind society's Disease of Despair. Let's find out what that sabotage is in the next lesson.

Bonus Content

Discover more about the neurobiology of your Stone-Age Tribe brain and the tools for you to manage stress and anxiety by going to www.ScienceofaHappyBrain.com

- Watch video how stress sabotages your happiness.
- Discover tools to overcome your brain's negativity bias.
- Learn three things you can begin to enact today to minimize stress and anxiety in your life.

LESSON THREE

SUFFERING IS A DISSATISFIED BRAIN

> An undisciplined mind leads to suffering. A
> disciplined mind leads to happiness.
> —the Dalai Lama

Why You Suffer

Have you ever found yourself overcome with pure pleasure during the early stages of romance? You know what I'm talking about—the burning passion and deep longing to be with the person who's the object of your desire. Now imagine it's been a few days since you've last seen each other and tonight you'll be reunited at long last. All week you've been preoccupied about how wonderful it's going to feel being in the presence of your love. It's the hour before your romantic dinner date. You get a call from your partner saying he or she is cancelling due to not feeling well. For over a week you were so anticipating this special dinner together that the sudden change of plans makes you so frustrated you want to scream. Sound familiar?

The reason I bet many of you can likely relate to this scenario is that during some point in your life you've experienced the emotional frenzy felt going from intense delight (the anticipation of pleasure) to great disappointment (the denial of pleasure). In whatever way you're deprived from an expected pleasure, your brain reacts precisely in the same manner—you suffer. That's exactly how evolution wants it to be. To be more precise, your brain is wired for dissatisfaction and suffering. Your dissatisfied brain became vital for human survival. Let's explore why suffering is a dissatisfied brain.

I really hate to do this, but I have more unpleasant news for you. As a strategy to promote survival, evolution not only wired your brain to favor stress over happiness; it's also the reason behind your suffering. It's hopefully becoming clear to you how nature allowed for your Stone-Age Tribe brain to evolve for survival. As you've just learned in the previous lesson, stress is a biological product of your brain and body. Suffering, on the other hand, is something you likely tend to view as an emotional or psychological product of your being. In this sense, both stress and suffering intrinsically connect your brain, body, and being.

What I want you to learn from this lesson is why suffering, like stress, simultaneously plays an evolutionary advantage for your survival and sabotage for your Happy Brain. I also intend to introduce how psychological suffering correlates with the biological functioning of your brain's pleasure and reward center and corresponds to a system in your brain known as the *dopaminergic-reward system*, all of which hijack your Happy Brain. Let's find out why.

Just as you discovered the necessity of stress as a tactic for survival through evolutionary biology, the same holds true for suffering. You wouldn't be the first to find this news astonishing. Many of you would agree a life of stress and suffering isn't exactly what you associate with a Happy Brain. To help you understand the origin of suffering and recognize its function for humanity's survival, let's explore it through another equally powerful lens of inquiry—not science, but spirituality. Yes, spirituality.

As an academic specializing in the convergence of science and spirituality, I find many of the world's ancient traditions, contemplative practices, and faiths have advanced timeless wisdom on the nature of human suffering—not to mention, the strategies for achieving happiness. I want you to appreciate how science and spirituality are complementary means for you to achieve a Happy Brain. It's precisely the reason why exploring your Happy Brain among the world's spiritual paths is an integral aspect for your Happiness course. Even as someone who's a strong advocate for science, I'd rightfully say spiritual masters and religious leaders throughout history have equally espoused the origins of human suffering and the means to reduce it.

Many religions have advanced teachings on how to alleviate suffering in the world. There is, however, one religion I'd say that has built its entire foundation upon and dedicated thousands of years of inquiry into investigating this fundamental and universal aspect of the human condition. That religion is Buddhism, and its founder is the Buddha. This is more than just my own opinion here, as I feel it would be a statement shared by other scholars in the field of comparative religious studies. To be clear, I'm in no way attempting to advocate for the superiority of Buddhism or its teachings over those found in other religions. I, myself, was not raised a Buddhist, and I rightfully believe why all religious traditions provide core aspects of wisdom and value for many people.

What I'm advancing—as someone who holds authority in and teaches courses in religion and philosophy—is how no other world's major religion has explored the causes behind human suffering to the extent of Buddhism. True, it's certainly valid to say other spiritual masters, saints, and prophets have endured severe forms of suffering in their own right. But what makes the Buddha unique? Why does Buddhism offer such profound wisdom on the nature of suffering? The answer is simple. Over 2,500 years ago, the Buddha established his entire philosophical teachings focused around answering one very basic question that has baffled and plagued humanity for eons: *Why do we suffer?*

The Buddha's ultimate goal was to create a strategy for you to experience the benefits of a Happy Brain by overcoming the human afflictions of anger, anxiety, and addiction. He did so by exposing the mental, psychological, emotional, and behavioral impediments that hijack your happiness. The Buddha was more than a philosopher or spiritual teacher; he was, and still remains, history's premiere behavioral psychologist.

Although the historical figure called the Buddha was born a prince, during his life, he witnessed and even endured his fair share of suffering. But the suffering he experienced was self-imposed. After rejecting his royal title and renouncing all worldly possessions, the former prince embarked for decades as a spiritual seeker wandering throughout India nearly twenty-five centuries ago on his quest for attaining spiritual enlightenment—you might even say, he was on a quest for human happiness. At one point, he nearly died from starvation and austere practices while on his mission. What made him do so? He undertook these actions to better understand and experience firsthand the nature of human suffering.

One day while in deep meditation, he reached an epiphany. The Buddha discovered the origin and location of suffering—the mind. That's correct. According to the Buddha, your suffering originates in your mind. The Buddha believed if suffering is the opposite of happiness, then the sabotages for your happiness equally originate in your mind. The Buddha squarely placed the accountability for your suffering not on some divine agent or external circumstances but revealed why your mind exists in a conditioned state of suffering. The Buddha advocates that you're deluded by the perceptual illusions created by your mind that ensnare you into a life of suffering. The Buddha revealed thousands of years ago what the field of behavioral psychology affirms today—the key to cease your suffering and to claim your happiness starts with shifting your thoughts, actions, and perceptions.

The Buddha's realization is brilliant. You're the agent of your own suffering and the master of your own happiness. In order to achieve happiness, you must first awaken from this mental delusional state that tricks you into a life of suffering. You unknowingly create and perpetuate your own suffering. The Buddha came to realize that because you're the author of your own suffering, you also hold the power to change it. Most of all, it takes effort, discipline, and patience. The Buddha would agree—happiness takes practice.

The word Buddha literally means "the awakened one." In the jargon of today's Millennials, the Buddha was truly "woke." According to Buddhism, being "woke" means how everyone can become awakened to the truth and liberated from suffering. You all have the potential to become "Buddhas" and become "woke" in your own right. As the Buddha rightfully wished, "May all beings have happy minds." He knew everyone could achieve happiness, despite one's mental state of delusion and the obstacles the mind sometimes creates to hijack it. Here's the essence and veracity behind the Buddha's benediction.

The Buddha's wisdom is simple and, yet, so profound. He arrived at a very startling conclusion about the essential nature of human behavior by formulating some truths about the human condition—all life is based in suffering, and more importantly, there exists a cure to cease suffering. This is where language and context become important. While you may think of suffering in its physical form, the Buddha implied the concept of suffering was more than mere physical pain or discomfort.

While the Buddha lived during a period of history when people endured tremendous physical hardship, he was far more concerned about the nature of *existential suffering*. The Buddha wanted to know what is it that makes life hard. He wasn't inquiring about what causes the agony endured from a broken bone or shattered lung, but more so he investigated the anguish caused from a broken heart or a shattered life. The Buddha aimed to discover why you experience psychological and emotional forms of suffering and how you can eradicate the root causes of suffering from your life.

To reiterate a very important point, the Buddha firmly teaches your suffering originates in your mind. This is the other reason why I choose Buddhism as the religion *par excellence* and the lens through which to examine the nature of human suffering. It's how Buddhist psychology—yes, that really is a field of academic study—and the Buddha's teachings elegantly align with the science of a Happy Brain. Without the benefit of medical technology or the ability to peer inside the human brain, the Buddha formulated a model for suffering that astonishingly resembles findings currently reached in the disciplines of brain science and evolutionary psychology.

The Buddha came to the conclusion that the origin of your suffering is powerfully linked to your insatiable craving for pleasure and your perpetual aversion to pain. More pleasure, less pain. The Buddha understood pain isn't the only culprit for your suffering—

pleasure equally plays a part. Are you surprised? While it's probably clear why you don't want to experience pain, how did the Buddha conjecture your pursuit of pleasure leads to suffering? He keenly observed human behavior and deciphered the mystery of the mind.

The laboratory the Buddha used to formulate his hypothesis on the origin of human suffering—and essentially what sabotages your happiness—is the human psyche, the mental realm of thoughts, and the nature of human experience. Everything the Buddha discovered about the essence of suffering nearly 2,500 years ago appears to correspond with what's presently known about your brain's pleasure and reward circuits. Just as your brain's stress-response system became crucial for survival, studies in evolutionary biology indicate how your brain's pleasure and reward system functioned as an indispensable aspect for you to survive. No other religion comes closer to contemporary findings about the functionality of your brain and the mechanisms in your mind than Buddhism. Here's how your lesson on Buddhism and your Happy Brain unfolds.

I Can't Get No Satisfaction

I want to share with you the wisdom of one of history's greatest and most famous psychologists—the Buddha—and why Buddhism is the religion that continues to affirm what research on the brain reveals about your quest for happiness. While designating the Buddha a psychologist may sound a little far-fetched, here's the reason why it's a fair assessment.

I find it interesting how the words *psychiatrist* and *psychologist* both bear the Ancient Greek word *psyche*. While there's a tendency to translate it as "mind," *psyche* originally expressed to the early Greeks the notion of "soul, spirit, or inner being." Thus, the literal translation of the word *psychiatrist* is "healer of the soul" and a *psychologist* means "one who studies the soul." Just as today's doctors evolved from ancient shamans and priests, current medicine distantly reflects humanity's ancient link to the religious and spiritual. Although, modern psychiatry and psychology reject the existence of the soul, in many ways these fields are gradually beginning to recognize the spiritual roots of suffering.

Despite the marvelous medical advancements in mapping the brain and exploring the neural correlates of mental illness, medicine can no longer neglect a significant aspect of what makes you human—your spiritual nature. Just to remember, spirituality refers to the universal human drive to find a sense of meaning, purpose, and identity in life and doesn't necessarily have to be associated with any particular religion. It's for this reason, why it's valid to refer to the Buddha as a preeminent psychologist. The Buddha keenly understood and revealed that the origin of suffering exists in your psyche—the inner terrain of your being.

Here's one of the earliest teachings by the Buddha that backs up what I just stated. Upon reaching Enlightenment, the Buddha delivered his first sermon. He revealed: "Life is suffering. There's a cause to suffering. There exist three poisons of suffering—craving, aversion, and confusion. Most importantly, there exists a path to cease suffering."

What's truly fascinating about the Buddha's three poisons of suffering is how they align to the three afflictions you're learning that are at the core of society's Disease of Despair. The first poison of suffering—craving—is essentially *addiction*. The insatiable craving for sensations that generate pleasure is the basis for addiction. The next poison—aversion—aligns to *anxiety* when you fear and wish to avoid circumstances in life that yield stress and pain. While the third poison of suffering—confusion—manifests as the *anger* you experience in life when you're driven to pain or are denied pleasure. Whether it's the Buddha's three poisons of craving, aversion, and confusion or the three afflictions of anger, anxiety, and addiction, they all expose the deeper state of existential human suffering.

In the context of the science of a Happy Brain when I say *suffering*, I'm really talking about how your brain evolved for you never to be satisfied with what you currently have or what presently is. Why do you suffer? Because evolution prefers your dissatisfied brain over a satisfied one. No matter how hard you try, you're always seeking more satisfaction. Cue the famous lyrics from The Rolling Stones: "*I can't get no satisfaction. And I try and I try and I try.*"

If there's one Buddhist term you ever learn in your life relevant for your Happiness course on the nature of suffering and your Happy Brain, that word is *duhkha*. The word *duhkha* first appears in the ancient Sanskrit language of India over 3,000 years ago. While *duhkha* is often translated into English by the word *suffering*, in actuality, there really is no precise equivalent for this word in English. While the Sanskrit word *duhkha* appears frequently in the much earlier religious texts in Hinduism that predate Buddhism by several centuries, a closer semantic scrutiny of the word in Buddhist scripture implies *duhkha* conveys something akin to the English word *dissatisfaction*. [5]

Even though *dissatisfaction* still doesn't fully express the nuances behind this important Buddhist term, the idea of *dissatisfaction* rings much more closely to what the Buddha implied behind the concept of *duhkha* thousands of years ago. It's why I prefer using the word *dissatisfaction* than the usually translated word *suffering* when teaching about this fundamental Buddhist concept. What exactly did the Buddha say about *duhkha*? A lot.

The Buddha observed *duhkha* originates in your mind. He surmised *duhkha* is the dissatisfaction derived from desiring fleeting pleasures and avoiding inevitable pain. It's why the Buddha precisely conceptualized *duhkha* as your insatiable thirst, hunger, or craving for situations that minimize pain and maximize pleasure. *Duhkha* is grounded in your mind's attraction to pleasure and aversion from pain.

The Buddha further came to realize that both your pain and your pleasure are temporary states. Pain and pleasure are impermanent. To understand the significance behind the Buddhist concept of impermanence and how it relates to the idea of suffering, here's a Buddhist joke you might enjoy: *How do you make a happy person*

---

[5] While the word *duhkha* is the common term in many Buddhist texts composed in the Sanskrit language, the word *dukka* is the term employed in the Pali language. Both *duhkha* and *dukka* convey the same meaning.

become sad, and a sad person become happy? Just say, "What you're feeling will soon pass."

What this punch line implies is how the Buddha realized nothing lasts forever—both good times and bad times are temporary experiences. Both pain and pleasure are fleeting sensations in your fluctuating mind, but in the moment your mind deceives you into thinking these states are permanent. In the case of pain, you suffer when you forget painful experiences are only temporary; in the case of pleasure, you suffer when you forget pleasurable experiences are momentary. In both situations, suffering ensues. This is *duhkha*— the existential suffering that results from your mind being trapped in the illusion of permanence and attached to the temporary emotional state of life's situations that produce pain or pleasure. The Buddha understood that in each of these situations the result is the same— you experience *duhkha*.

If you recall, the Buddha mentioned there were three forms of poison inherent in *duhkha*—craving, aversion, and confusion. This is how the Buddha explained it in the context of impermanence. You *crave* pleasurable experiences when they're gone. You're *averse* to painful experiences when they're present. You become *confused* in both of these situations by forgetting how sensations of pain and pleasure are temporary by nature. In all of these instances, the Buddha believed failing to accept the impermanence of situations in life is the cause of your suffering—your dissatisfaction in life. If the Buddha were alive today, he'd declare unequivocally that society's Disease of Despair is identical to the Buddhist disease of *duhkha*, as both derive from human suffering. So how does *duhkha* connect to your Happy Brain?

With regard to your brain, if pain drives stress, pleasure delivers suffering. As you learned in the previous lesson, pain activates your brain's stress-response system, but what about your pursuit of pleasure? Let's explore specifically how the Buddhist concept of *duhkha* relates to your brain's drive for pleasure, why it became an evolutionary strategy for survival, and how it ultimately undermines your Happy Brain.

When it comes to experiencing pleasure, the Buddha intimately understood how *duhkha* results from the dissatisfaction that inevitably ensues when the object of pleasure is denied from you or—even worse—when the experience of pleasure is gone, and you crave more of it. While there exists a distinction between experiencing pleasure and happiness, let's save that for a later lesson. For the moment, let's focus on your brain's primal pleasure circuits and the neurobiology behind why experiencing pleasure became vital for human survival and how it connects to the Buddhist concept of *duhkha*. If pain is associated with your brain's stress-response system, then pleasure and reward are connected with your brain's dopaminergic-reward system. In the context of Buddhist psychology, think of *duhkha* as the spiritual counterpart to the scientific dopaminergic-reward system. If you're game, here's another experiential exercise I want you to try in order to help you appreciate how the experience of *duhkha*, your pursuit of pleasure, and your brain's dopaminergic-reward system align.

I want you to bring to mind your favorite dessert. For me it's definitely anything chocolate. But whatever that dessert is for you, get a clear mental picture of it. Once you've done so, imagine yourself on the verge of taking the first long-awaited bite of your dessert. Even though the dessert isn't actually there, feel the anticipation of what it's like to savor the pleasure from delighting in your favorite dessert. Now if it's possible, close your eyes for the next ten seconds as you engage in this mental exercise. Did you actually feel your saliva glands activate or even your stomach rumble from the very thought of eating your dessert?

Even though the dessert isn't physically present for you, the mere pleasurable memory from and anticipation for eating the dessert trick your brain. Every previous experience from eating your favorite dessert triggers your brain's dopaminergic-reward system by releasing the neurotransmitter dopamine into your body. There's no surprise how the feeling of pleasure or anticipation for pleasurable experiences is wired into your mind and memory. If you've ever experienced a food craving or dealt with any form of addiction, you know exactly how this works. Now that you've understood how memory from and anticipation for pleasure activate your brain's release of dopamine, now comes the really interesting—and cruel—next part of this exercise for you to do.

Go ahead and bring to mind one more time your yummy dessert. Now imagine you're at a restaurant, and you immediately eye your all-time favorite dessert on the menu. Throughout the whole meal you've got one thing on your mind—anticipating how awesome it's going to be relishing every morsel of your dessert. Your server comes to take away your main course and asks if you'd like any dessert. Of course you do! You tell your server precisely the dessert you've been craving the moment you saw it on the menu. Your server looks at you with disappointment and confesses, "I'm so sorry but the kitchen just ran out of that particular dessert a minute ago. In fact, the table next to you just got the very last order." You turn to see the last serving of your favorite dessert being eaten. It gets worse. The person only takes two bites—from what you were hoping to have been your dessert—before asking the server to take back the remaining uneaten portion. Aaaagh!

So, what's your immediate and instinctive reaction to this scenario? Dismay at the restaurant for running out of dessert, frustration you won't get to enjoy it, jealousy of seeing the person eat what should be your dessert, contempt at that person for wasting the dessert, or stupidity for your waiting too long to order the dessert? Whatever emotion you feel—frustration, disappointment, jealousy, contempt, or self-loathing—this is a natural reaction for your Stone-Age Tribe brain in the moment.

In a "dog-eat-dog world"—or maybe in today's "dessert-eat-dessert world"—your Stone-Age Tribe brain still views life through the lens of strife, scarcity, and suspicion. Being deprived from that last piece of your favorite dessert instinctively triggers your brain's stress-response, just as it did back in the Stone-Age when an enemy stole that pile of berries you just spent hours gathering. In both scenarios, your Stone-Age Tribe brain perceives being denied what you claim to be rightfully yours as a threat to survival. Even though for your ancient ancestor not getting to eat the pile of berries could mean starvation and death, not getting to eat your dessert one night only inflicts upset and anxiety. This again is the foible of your Stone-

Age Tribe brain. It forgets it's no longer 10,000 BCE. It tricks you into behaving as if you're still living in the Stone Age.

Now, let's try something else. Imagine you've paid your bill, you've driven home, and you're about to go to bed. But the emotional charge from still being denied the pleasure from eating your dessert still stews in your mind. Even though you can't change the situation from what happened at the restaurant, you're still upset you didn't get your dessert. While your Stone-Age Tribe brain's initial reaction at the restaurant rightfully produced stress, the Buddha would identify your residual emotional response to the situation as a classic example of *duhkha*.

In this case, even though the anguish over what transpired at the restaurant happened an hour ago, your mind still chooses to suffer. Your body is still reacting from the spike in cortisol that results from attachment to your anger and anxiety from being denied pleasure. Your mind is still attached to the craving for eating that dessert. And that's the key. Being emotionally attached to situations you cannot change or have passed results in *duhkha*. The Buddha taught that you suffer when things don't go your way. Suffering perpetuates from being attached to impermanent experiences. Despite the situation having long passed, you choose to stew in your suffering. The key word is *choose*.

Here's the main point—if stress is an involuntary and immediate reaction from your Stone-Age Tribe brain, perpetuated suffering is your own choosing. The Buddha figured this out and came to the conclusion that the psychological suffering you experience in life is self-created. Because it's self-generated, you have the ability to stop it. In a nutshell, this is what the Buddha taught and what Buddhist psychology reveals—if stress is an evolutionary product of your neurobiology that's impossible to eliminate, suffering isn't. Since suffering is something you can learn to control, Buddhism correctly affirms how your happiness is equally under your control. *Duhkha* sabotages your Happy Brain. The Buddha believed that realizing this truth liberates you from suffering and is the foundation for achieving your Happy Brain.

This is what the Buddha knew to be the source of your suffering—the dissatisfaction from not getting what you want in the moment. I guess it wasn't the Rolling Stones but the Buddha who first got it right: *I can't get no satisfaction.*

This Is Your Brain on Sex

Let's examine in more detail what the Buddha uncovered thousands of years ago about *duhkha* and the nature of suffering through the lens of contemporary brain science. What Buddhism and the Buddha figured out—millennia before what studies in brain science currently reveal—is how your brain evolved for you to seek out pleasurable experiences. When these situations are thwarted, denied, or gone, you suffer—more precisely, you experience dissatisfaction. That's the gist of it. Knowing human behavior functions in this manner, why would your brain develop to be wired for pleasure and make you susceptible to dissatisfaction once the sensation of pleasure is gone? The answer again has to do with survival and how your brain's dopaminergic-reward system governs your motivation, anticipation, and reward of pleasure.

Let's use another example many of you likely can relate to—sex. I think most of you would agree how consensual sex is a highly pleasurable event. Aside from the pleasure you get from it, sex has another function. Sex simultaneously serves a biological, psychological, social, and even a spiritual reason for why so many greatly enjoy partaking in this pleasurable activity. This Bio-Psycho-Socio-Spiritual model was introduced earlier and will be explored in greater detail in the next lessons. For the moment, let's look at human sexuality through this Bio-Psycho-Socio-Spiritual lens.

Regardless of your personal preference for enjoying consensual sex, it does more than just bring you pleasure. Evolution's original goal for sex—specifically as a reproductive act—is to assist in the survival of the species. Just because heterosexual intercourse became nature's optimal method for biological reproduction, sex in all its glorious permutations equally serves a psychological, social, and spiritual purpose. The *biological motivation* behind sex is reproduction; the *psychological motivation* is the anticipation of pleasure; the *social motivation* is the reward of intimacy; while the *spiritual motivation* is the communion of love.

Sex is sure one great way to experience pleasure, and it's the reason why your brain loves it. Sexual pleasure generated from arousal and orgasm is intensely powerful and activates your brain's dopaminergic-reward system—among other systems in the brain. Believe it or not, people have volunteered to be placed in fMRI machines to get their brains scanned in real time while having an orgasm. Try getting that image out of your mind. What these studies found is how sex, like anything associated with your brain's dopaminergic-reward system, is processed as pleasurable experiences.

It's why activities like eating, sleeping, and even urgently relieving yourself of bodily waste can all produce sensations of pleasure. But what unites all these biological activities is they enhance your chances for getting to live another day. Digestion, recuperation, and elimination increase your odds for survival. Nature is again very clever. In order to get you to continue eating, sleeping, and evacuating your bladder and bowels, it made all of these activities produce sensations of pleasure in your brain. If these experiences weren't pleasurable, you'd have no desire to continue engaging in them. You'd eventually die from starvation, exhaustion, or constipation.

Nature ensured your craving of pleasurable experiences guaranteed survival. Once again, this might seem like another one of nature's idea of a sadistic joke. While the pursuit of pleasurable experiences—like food, sex, and sleep—is wired into your neurobiology, your brain equally evolved to experience the dissatisfaction that ensues when the pleasure is gone. Why would nature be so cruel to you by wanting you to suffer in such a way? Survival, survival, survival! Here's the ploy behind nature's sinister strategy around sex.

Sex is one powerful example how your brain's dopaminergic-reward system governs motivation, anticipation, and reward. The first time you ever experienced sexual arousal or orgasm—again, assuming the experience was safe and voluntary—insanely large amounts of dopamine got released into your body. The sensation was so intense, you felt motivated to do it again, again, and again. Irrespective of how arousal or orgasm is experienced or the form of sex you engage in, it equally activates your brain's dopaminergic-reward system. If nature developed sexual intercourse to occur without experiencing the intense pleasure from orgasm, it's highly unlikely you'd have any motivation for sex. No sex, no reproduction. No reproduction, extinction of the species.

The primary function behind the sensation of pleasure is for your brain to motivate you for an anticipated reward. Once again, it's helpful to think about the idea of pleasure—especially as a function for survival—via the perspective of your Stone-Age Tribe brain. Project yourself back thousands of years ago to a time when enduring unrelenting strife and scarcity was the harsh reality of life. Seeking food, warmth, sex, or a safe place to sleep was no guarantee. Meeting all of these desires required active involvement. The alternative to not fulfilling these desires was quite simple—death to you, but more crucially, the extinction of the human species.

In the context of the science of a Happy Brain, "Rewards are defined as those objects, which we will work to acquire through allocation of time, energy, or effort; that is, any object or goal that we seek. Rewards are crucial for individual and support elementary processes such as drinking, eating and reproduction."[6] Rewarding you with pleasure in the form of a big boost of dopamine is how your brain establishes a neurochemical incentive by reinforcing actions that promote survival.

As noted UCLA social neuroscientist, Matthew Lieberman, aptly puts it, "In simple terms, we gravitate toward things the brain has learned to associate with dopaminergic release."[7] The dopaminergic-reward system signals to your brain dedicating the time to forage, hunt, or look for a suitable mate will ultimately reward you with

6. Oscar Arias-Carrión, Maria Stamelou, Eric Murillo-Rodríguez, Manuel Menéndez-González, and Ernst Pöppel, "Dopaminergic reward system: a short integrative review," *International Archives of Medicine* 2010, 3:24.

7. Matthew Lieberman, *Social: Why Our Brains Are Wired to Connect* (Broadway Books, 2014), 93.

pleasure. The pursuit of pleasure is hardwired into your brain for survival. Focusing on pleasure is instinctual for your Stone-Age Tribe brain; finding happiness is not.

Your brain's built-in anticipatory reward mechanism for motivating you to continue actions, no matter their challenge or stress, is the evolutionary origin of pleasure. This is why humans need pleasure and how it got wired into your brain—it became a crucial strategy for survival of the species. In the absence of dopaminergic neurons in your brain, there'd be no incentive for you to continue to eat, have sex, sleep, bear children, and—most importantly—survive. In this way, the neurotransmitter dopamine governs your behavior behind motivation, anticipation, and reward.

Become the Buddha

Bringing it back to Buddhism, what the Buddha got right nearly 2,500 years ago is how suffering—manifesting as *duhkha*—is embedded into the human equation as another primal impediment for experiencing your Happy Brain. Neuroscience recently has revealed how your intrinsic drive for pleasure—exhibiting as the dopaminergic-reward system—is wired into your brain that the Buddha proclaimed was the source of your suffering. Again, with regard to suffering, both Buddhism and brain science really mean the dissatisfaction that ensues when you're denied having pleasurable experiences or when they're no longer there. Both *duhkha* and the dopaminergic-reward system function as an evolutionary strategy for survival.

I hope you're equally impressed as I am how the Buddha arrived at this realization thousands of years before the advent of brain science and medical scans. What Buddhist psychology investigates is highly relevant for you today, just as much as it was thousands of years ago when the Buddha discovered these truths. It's in the terrain of your thoughts—your *psyche*—where you cease *duhkha* and also achieve your happiness.

The bottom line is this: Evolution primed your brain to be in a perpetual state of dissatisfaction by craving more pleasure—whether deriving from food, sex, or an artificial substance. Actions and behaviors that promote survival become associated with pleasure. Doing so forces you to seek out and continue these experiences, as they allow for you to live and reproduce, thereby, ensuring continuity of the species. As extraordinary and empowering this evolutionary aspect of your Stone-Age Tribe brain became for survival of the species, for you it sadly still hijacks your happiness.

Just as your brain's stress-response system became crucial for survival, you've learned how stress equally can sabotage your happiness. The same holds true for the dopaminergic-reward system. Although evolution wired your brain to crave and quench the thirst for pleasure, the very same strategy hijacks your happiness. For humans living today, the necessity for experiencing pleasure still behaves as a functional mechanism for survival. The danger exists when your drive for pleasure becomes unstoppable or unrelenting, and it morphs into an addiction. Your brain's dopaminergic-reward system equally governs your pursuit of pleasure and generates addictive behaviors. But there's good news.

Let's return to the Dalai Lama's opening quote of this lesson: "An undisciplined mind leads to suffering. A disciplined mind leads to happiness." Let's examine this statement in the context of what you've just learned. While there are poetic parallels between Buddhism and brain science, when it comes to the nature of your suffering, there's one notable similarity. The Buddha always knew that even though you may be conditioned for suffering, you aren't imprisoned by it. You can become the Buddha—you can awaken and become liberated from *duhkha*. Despite suffering being self-generated, you have the power to change your perspective on the circumstances in your life. How do you become the Buddha? It begins by disciplining your mind and training your brain. Choosing to do nothing perpetuates your suffering; acquiring the skills for your Happy Brain requires discipline. Every one of you has the ability to become a Buddha and awaken from the slumber of your suffering. The Buddha knew this. It's now a realization advanced by behavioral psychology.

While Buddhism refers to suffering as an aspect of your mind, neuroscience affirms how suffering is wired into your brain. If the Buddha were alive today and had access to all the scientific research on the nature of human suffering, he'd agree how it takes more than just your disciplined mind, it takes your disciplined brain. A disciplined brain is a Happy Brain. Your Happy Brain generates a happy outlook on life. Your happy outlook on life is the key to achieving a happy world.

Despite evolution's primary goal for survival of the species by wiring stress and suffering into the human equation, the human brain had one proverbial "ace up its sleeve." What is this one extraordinary feat humans possessed to become the predominant species on the planet? Stay tuned and find out in your next lesson.

Bonus Content

- Go to www.ScienceofaHappyBrain.com and explore why your disciplined brain is your Happy Brain.
- Watch video on the Buddha's views on why you suffer.
- Discover how society programs you to perpetuate suffering—and what actions you can take to stop it.

LESSON FOUR

THE HAPPINESS EQUATION

It's important to find your tribe.

—RuPaul

To Socialize Is to Survive, to Tribe Is to Thrive

When I was five, my parents decided to relocate from our home in the charming countryside of England to the western suburbs of Chicago in order to pursue their medical careers. I remember to this very day my sense of what it felt from the moment the plane landed at Chicago O'Hare airport to arriving at the motel where we temporarily stayed for the weekend. My child's brain absorbed every detail of the experience with full fascination. I remember wondering to myself: *Why do the people here talk funny? Why is the taxi guy driving on the wrong side of the road? When do we get to go back home to England? I miss my bedroom. I want to see my friends.*

Like any young child would be, I felt a mixture of confusion and curiosity to my new environment. Despite the normal challenges that my transition of moving to a different country posed—from having to make new friends to quickly adapting to speak with an American accent—there was one constant during that period of my life that allowed me to thrive and be happy. It was the certainty of knowing that I had the unconditional love and protection from my parents to ensure the fullness of my future life in America.

You can often take it for granted that without the support and safety from others—your family, friends, neighbors, and partner—your life would be one of strife and struggle. Like all humans, you are unquestionably a social creature that evolved for community and connection—for tribe. The instinctive drive to bond with others and to band into social groups continues to be a fundamental feature of human behavior. Tribe remains central to the Happiness Equation of humanity. Allow me to reveal what this formula is and how it equates with your Happy Brain.

Having now learned about nature's ploy to sabotage your Happy Brain by promoting stress and suffering as a strategy for survival, let's explore one of the most amazing aspects of research to come out of brain science as it pertains to your quest for happiness. What I want to convey to you in this lesson is what appears to be the most credible argument why achieving your Happy Brain is possible. Moreover, without this one fundamental feature of your brain, the chances for humans having become the predominant species on the planet might not have ever happened.

Do you remember the exercise from a couple of lessons ago when I had you close your eyes and imagine yourself going back to 10,000 BCE to the Stone Age? At the end of this paragraph, I'd like for you to close your eyes again. Envision yourself in this same scenario—alone and terrified wandering around the wild terrains of ancient Earth. Your Stone-Age Tribe brain is on heightened alert. Every minute of the day your life is under legitimate threats from hungry predators, darkness, starvation, and fatigue. Still pretty scary, huh? But this time, I want you to close your eyes for a few seconds and to visualize you have one other able-bodied person you trust by your side. Do you think your odds for survival will increase by having just one more person there with you for protection?

Now suppose you have two, five, ten, twenty, fifty other people who are collectively looking out for you and each other's safety and security. Do you think your chances for living another day just exponentially increased? Of course, it would, right?

What this valuable exercise for you imparts is how the powerful ability for your ancient ancestors to band into social groups for the sake of survival was humanity's secret weapon against beating out nature. If evolution primed your brain for stress and suffering, we humans responded to nature and came up with our own clever strategy to enhance survival—tribe. This exercise also affirms the importance of the "Tribe" aspect of the term Stone-Age Tribe brain.

In the past two lessons, you saw how the "Stone-Age" component of your Stone-Age Tribe brain focused on how stress and suffering became favorable for survival. Likewise, the "Tribe" portion of this term expresses how social bonding and group cooperation became another powerful tactic for survival. Allow me to explain how it all fits together.

Your Stone-Age Tribe brain equates survival with happiness. To be clear, when I say "happiness" in the context of your Stone-Age Tribe brain, it's the joy and relief for just getting to live another day. Because tribe ensures survival, tribe becomes a tactic for your Happy Brain. This is the main point I want you to remember for this lesson that underscores the powerful motto of your Happy Brain—*to socialize is to survive, to tribe is to thrive*. Tribe is the quintessential key to your Happy Brain. It remains just as true today, as it did millennia ago for your ancient ancestors.

What medical science wasn't cognizant of just as recently as a few decades ago, research from brain science and behavioral health is shedding a striking new light onto the nature of the human condition and the science of a Happy Brain. This discovery is the revolutionary concept of the "Social Brain" hypothesis and the accompanying Bio-Psycho-Socio-Spiritual model. This lesson reveals why coalescing into tribes became an evolutionary adaptation for survival and how your Happy Brain must be viewed in the proper context of its biological, psychological, social, and spiritual function. Let's start by exploring the science behind why evolution discovered your Happy Brain is a Social Brain.

One extraordinary—yet still largely unexplored and undervalued—discovery to come out of brain science research over the past few decades is the "Social Brain" model of human development. It's the revolutionary idea how your brain evolved fundamentally as a social organ as a strategy for survival. Of course, the concept of the

Social Brain doesn't diminish nor deny many other groundbreaking findings that have been and are rapidly emerging from the field of neuroscience. Rather, the Social Brain model of human development is one that bears tremendous significance to address the complex array of issues facing society today. The Social Brain model is also a novel approach to explore the science of a Happy Brain. So how did the idea of the Social Brain develop?

The first clue that led scientists to conjecture the idea of the Social Brain was the curious observation why we humans (along with many other primates such as chimpanzees and gorillas) have a disproportionately larger neo-cortex—the part of your brain that gives you a big, protruding crown and forehead—in relation to body size when compared to most other mammals. Robin Dunbar, considered to be the pioneer behind what is known as the "Social Brain Hypothesis," originally argued "that primates need large brains because their form of sociality is much more complex than that of other species. This does not mean that they live in larger social groups than other species of animals (in fact, they don't), but rather that their groups have a more complex structure."[8]

Of course, other factors such as the diet eaten by early humans and the harsher climate experienced during this time might also have attributed to the development of a larger brain. But the one argument that stands at the foundation for the Social Brain hypothesis is how humans required larger brains to navigate the complex array of social relationships and process the tremendous amount of cognitive information required to live and function in large communal groups. Being part of a tribe required early humans to develop bigger brains, in contrast to the smaller brain size of other species that lack the social complexity of humans.

But there's something unique about your brain you need to know that differentiates it from the brains of other primates that provides another explanation for the "Social Brain" hypothesis— the link between the size of the human brain and the duration of

8. Robin I. M. Dunbar, "The Social Brain Hypothesis and Human Evolution," Online Publication Date: Mar 2016. DOI: 10.1093/acrefore/9780190236557.013.44.

pregnancy. For the case of most other primates—such as chimpanzees or gorillas—their brains fully develop in size inside the mother's womb before birth. From the perspective of biology and as a strategy for survival of the species, you can understand why it would be an advantage for a baby to be born with a fully-grown brain. This is the situation for the majority of mammals and primates.

What you need to know, this isn't the case for human babies. It's been suggested that compared to other primates, a human baby is actually born six to nine months prematurely—that is, the full development of a human baby's brain continues after a mother gives birth. Why would that be the case, since it's clearly not a strategy for survival? Just ask any woman who's given birth. A fully developed brain requires a larger head. The larger the size of a baby's head, the more it jeopardizes the baby's passing through the mother's birth canal.

So how does this biological abnormality in human pregnancy relate to the idea of the Social Brain? By having human babies be born several months too soon—when compared to brain size and gestation period of other mammals—humans require considerably more bonding and nurturing at birth than other primates. This higher degree of vulnerability that human babies experience, due to being born prematurely and with brains still growing in size after birth, provides another intriguing explanation as to why humans are biologically wired for connection and what makes every one of you intensely social creatures. The other option—having babies remain in the womb for several more months and being born with a full-sized brain would've risked the lives of the mother and the baby during delivery. So, this is nature's trade-off. A shorter human gestation period demands greater social attachment at birth for the newborn that eventually leads to more complex socialization for the human species. Voilà, you now have the Social Brain.

The Social Brain model is one that's rapidly gaining credence and attention by a growing number of brain science researchers. The premise behind the Social Brain concept is again rather simple—the highly elaborate social networks your early human ancestors had to navigate through as a strategy for enhancing survival fundamentally shaped your brain to become the Social Brain it is today.

My friend and psychologist colleague, Lou Cozolino, echoes this idea when saying, "One thing is that the brain is a social organ, and that's an incredible discovery over the last twenty years or so. Because we tend to think about the brain as an organ like other organs, but the brain evolved really to connect with other brains. So the fact that the brain is a social organ gives us an understanding of why we are all connected."[9] While the evolutionary argument how the Social Brain evolved appears valid, what follows is the pivotal study in 2003 that boosted credibility for the Social Brain model. This remarkable research revealed something unexpected on how your brain processes and regulates pain.

Pain Is the Same in Your Brain

In recent years, remarkable breakthroughs in medical technology have enabled scientists to peer inside the brain in real time without invasive surgery to reveal the inner workings of your neurobiology. Through highly detailed imaging techniques, such as fMRI and PET scans, we've discovered more about your human brain in the past ten years than we have in the past ten centuries. Yup, we are living in what I call the "Decade of the Brain." It's the advent of these sophisticated brain-imaging machines that has recently provided one of the strongest pieces of evidence as to why you're endowed with your Social Brain. More specifically, it reveals the science why your Social Brain is your Happy Brain.

Thanks to the marvels of technology, scans reveal how your brain contains neural mechanisms for you to register the pain from loss, isolation, and abandonment similarly to physical pain. The following image reveals how this system operates in your brain.

---

9. Lou Cozolino, "The Brain Is a Social Organ," *Capella University*, May 27, 2011.

Image 1

Exhibit 1: Social and Physical Pain Produce Similar Brain Responses

Brain scans captured through functional magnetic resonance imaging (fMRI) show the same areas associated with distress, whether caused by social rejection or physical pain. The dorsal anterior cingulate cortex (highlighted at left) is associated with the degree of distress; the right ventral prefrontal cortex (highlighted at right) is associated with regulating the distress.

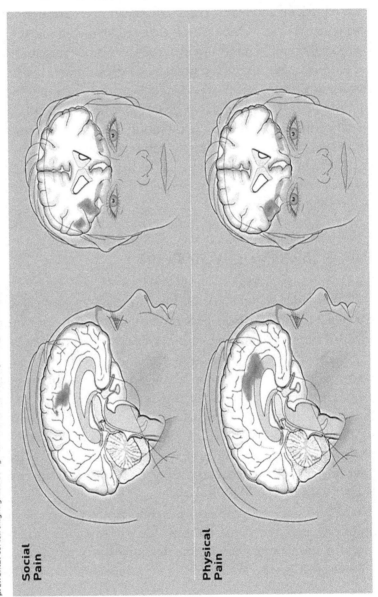

Social Pain

Physical Pain

Illustration: Samuel Valasco
Source: Eisenberger, Lieberman, and Williams, Science, 2003 (social pain images); Lieberman et al., "The Neural Correlates of Placebo Effects: A Disruption Account," Neuroimage, May 2004 (physical pain images)

If you're not someone who specializes in brain science, this discovery introduced the novel perspective of viewing your brain as a social organ. Here's why it becomes relevant for you. The top left half of the image shows an fMRI scan of the darkened area of your brain firing when you experience social pain—think getting dumped by your partner, a kid being bullied at school, a mother losing her baby, or a young child separated from a parent. The bottom left portion represents the area of your brain when you're in physical pain—think a migraine, toothache, or breaking a bone. Both images on the left—the top (social pain) and bottom (physical pain)—indicate the overlapping darkened regions of your brain firing when you experience distress, specifically the dorsal anterior cingulate cortex (dACC). The two right images are the shared region of your brain—the right ventromedial prefrontal cortex (rVMPC)—that co-regulate both physical and social pain.

An important caveat to note is this particular image itself doesn't indicate these are identical regions of your brain firing. Rather, what this image and this revolutionary study claim is the following—there exist *overlapping* regions of your brain that respond to social pain similarly as they do to physical pain, and the brain pathways that regulate your social distress appear to piggyback on the pathways that alleviate your physical distress.

What does this all mean? Why should you care? What does it have to do with your Happy Brain? Your brain associates the social pain felt when you're excluded, ostracized, neglected, or bullied by others similarly as the experience of physical pain. To put it another way: *Your brain processes and regulates the pain from broken bones and broken bonds in the same manner.* If you've ever agonized from the pain caused by the death of a loved one, a romantic breakup, watching others suffer, or even experiencing profound loneliness in your life, your Social Brain registers this pain, but it does *not* feel it in the same way.

While it's true the actual *sensation of pain* you feel from a broken bone isn't exactly as acute when your heart or morale is broken, both social pain and physical pain are *processed* by similar neural mechanisms in your brain. Here's the bottom line—your brain essentially evolved in such a way as to make it difficult to differentiate between social distress and physical distress. Pain is all the same to your brain. Why would your brain evolve in this manner to make you experience social and physical pain identically? The reason is something that astounded brain science researchers. The ability for your brain to evolve structures that share the same neural networks to process social pain and physical pain is yet another powerful strategy that favored human survival. UCLA neuropsychologist Naomi Eisenberger explains it perfectly,

> Indeed, although there is still much more to be explored, considerable evidence from human and animal research supports the hypothesis that physical and social pain rely on shared neural and neurochemical substrates. Although surprising in some ways, this co-opting of the primitive physical pain signal to indicate the possibility of broken social bonds highlights the critical role that social ties have played in the survival of our species. Continuing to explore the nature of this overlap may help us to more fully understand the depth of our social nature and to uncover the multiple ways in which our minds and bodies are inherently regulated by our social world.[10]

This is just another reason it becomes increasingly convincing why your brain is essentially a Social Brain wired for attachment and bonding with others. Furthermore, your primal Stone-Age Tribe brain and your Social Brain are intimately connected. As you learned in the last lessons, your Stone-Age Tribe brain is the primal layer of your brain that governs your behaviors around survival and self-preservation. If it's apparent your brain is essentially a Social

---

[10.] Naomi I. Eisenberger, "Social Pain and the Brain: Controversies, Questions, and Where to Go from Here," *Annual Review of Psychology* 2015. 66, 623.

Brain, you can think of your Stone-Age Tribe brain as the precursor to your more evolved Social Brain.

Your Stone-Age Tribe brain is focused primarily on beating and competing; your Social Brain is geared toward sharing and caring. Your Stone-Age Tribe brain is about the "me." Your Social Brain is about the "we." You'll explore this relationship of your Stone-Age Tribe brain and your Social Brain later in the lesson.

In truth, when I refer to your Social Brain, it's more accurate to call it the *Social Brain system* or the *social nervous system*, as it's a complex neurobiological network that developed in evolutionary stages over thousands of years and one that encompasses your brain, body, and being. The Social Brain system is a vast network that integrates your Stone-Age Tribe brain's stress-response mechanism (HPA-axis), the primal pain regulation system (opioid system), the seeking-reward system (dopaminergic-reward system), and the empathic response system (mirror-neuron system). These are some of the sub-components wired into your Stone-Age Tribe brain that link into the Social Brain system that will be particularly relevant in subsequent lessons as you learn how to cultivate your Happy Brain.

Additionally, your Social Brain is more than just a system regionalized to your physical brain, as it's one that links into other key systems within your body. If you've ever felt like you've been punched in the gut from learning your daughter was in a serious car accident or getting the unexpected news you're being fired from your job, it's your body's gut-brain (enteric system) at work. Research indicates the stress felt from social pain further leads to poorer health (immune system), a deficient microbiome (digestive system), and heart disease (cardiovascular system).

Social stress even negatively alters your metabolism, inflammation process, DNA function, longevity, memory, and cognition. Your Social Brain can also influence your state of being; your psychological sense of self-worth and confidence; your spiritual identity and faith; and your emotional experiences of feeling anger, shame, joy, and love. All of these aspects of your Social Brain confirm why the benefits of your Happy Brain are balance, longevity, and resilience. Your Social Brain regulates more than just your survival; it governs your Happy Brain.

The reason why your Social Brain is a unique prism through which to explore your Happy Brain is due to the evolutionary function how grouping into tribes played in human survival. Particularly, there's one equation I want to share with you that encapsulates how exactly your Social Brain, tribe, survival, and happiness intersect. I call it humanity's Happiness Equation. Let's now investigate this idea in this lesson of your Happiness course.

Your Happy Brain Is a Social Brain

If you recall from the last lesson, just as the human brain didn't come into its present form all of a sudden, the Social Brain system didn't emerge all at once. It evolved gradually in specific levels over the course of thousands of years of human history. There exists a primal and all-encompassing equation of your Social Brain that remains true for everybody today. It's the most relevant concept for understanding the science of a Happy Brain that you need to know.

The Happiness Equation
Attachment to Tribe = Life = Happy Brain
Abandonment from Tribe = Death = Despairing Brain

It's this Happiness Equation that unifies your Social Brain and your Stone-Age Tribe brain. Think of this formula as an archeological relic from human social evolution. In a harsh and hostile world where survival was paramount at all costs, there were really only two options available to your ancient ancestors—eat lunch tomorrow or be lunch today. It's precisely this stark choice between life and death how early humans realized why banding together into social groups—into tribes—increased not just your, but everyone's odds for eating lunch the next day. The Stone-Age Tribe brain is what made tribe possible and is the earliest stage of human neurobiology that would lead thousands of years later to the more complex Social

Brain system for humans today. If the primary goal for your Stone-Age Tribe brain is survival, experiencing attachment to your tribe made that possible. As more humans realized the functional strategy behind tribe and social solidarity, the creation of your Social Brain became a reality.

To put it in the simplest language—tribe made survival possible. Evolution tends to favor biological and behavioral traits that increase the chances for survival of the species. Just as the vital importance that tool usage, discovery of fire, and the domestication of animals enhanced survival, the ability for early humans to tighten into tribes is perhaps the most powerful adaptive tactic that enabled the human species to thrive in an unpredictable and treacherous world.

And here's the best part, folks. Those early humans who realized organizing into tribes enhanced the probability for survival passed on this functional strategy via their genes into every human who has ever lived on the planet, including you. If nothing else, this is the scientific rationale why tribe is a universal feature of humanity and the hidden key to your Happy Brain. Tribe is literally encoded into the fabric of your DNA. The necessity for tribe is wired into your brain. Knowing that you're part of a tribe makes your brain happy. The universal motto of your Happy Brain and of your Social Brain that remains true for everyone on the planet, who was, and ever will be born is: *To socialize is to survive, to tribe is to thrive.*

It's not just brain science research that attests to the universality of tribe. The need for community became a hallmark within all the world's religions. There exists strength and solidarity when you live in numbers versus being alone. You even witness this primal theme to tribe in media and entertainment. Before the rise in popularity of reality-TV, being "naked and afraid" was the reality of life, and still is for many people on the planet. Do you ever wonder the reason why survival-themed shows are so popular? They simultaneously target and trigger your Stone-Age Tribe brain's drive for survival and your Social Brain's craving for connection. If you've ever found yourself binge-watching shows such as *Naked and Afraid*™, *Survivor*™ or *Out of the Wild*™, it's both of these evolutionary levels of your brain taking in all the drama and tension with primal glee.

What these shows share in common are again the prevailing threats faced by your primal Stone-Age Tribe brain: *strife, scarcity, suspicion*. It's also why the contestants in these reality shows are all seeking the same three drives of your Stone-Age Tribe brain—*safety, security, stability*—whether these manifest in the form of food, shelter, or companionship. Remember, your Stone-Age Tribe brain is focused on one thing only—survival. The strategy for winning in the cruel contest of life thousands of years ago remains the same in the reality TV shows for contestants today. Those who best achieved survival had the best chance to win—whether that prize is making it to tomorrow or making out with a big check.

In the harsh contest of life, tribe is the winning strategy that ensured humanity grabbed the most coveted prize of all—survival. It's because of this universal drive for survival and the human longing for tribe, your Stone-Age Tribe brain eventually ushered in the necessity for your Social Brain. The development of your Social Brain and the strategy for aligning into tribes became the evolutionary tactic for competing in and winning the harshest reality show of all—life.

These reality shows basically reiterate the primal Happiness Equation that transcends the human condition. The ability for early humans to become part of a strong tribe accomplished more than ensuring survival and creation of your Social Brain; it became the basis for your Happy Brain. These ideas are encapsulated in the top half of the Happiness Equation:

Attachment to Tribe = Life = Happy Brain

But just as attachment to tribe becomes the foundation for life and promotes your Happy Brain, the opposite also bears truth. Abandonment from the tribe risks your chance of death and triggers your despairing brain. The dangers and damage that abandonment from tribe does to your brain can be viewed in the context of the Bio-Psycho-Socio-Spiritual model of stress and suffering.

Returning to the image of the brain earlier in this lesson, evolution allowed for overlapping regions of your brain to process and regulate all forms of pain. To put it in simple terms, experiencing abandonment from your tribe or social exclusion causes your brain to process this state of social pain as physical pain. Being part of a tribe and enjoying strong social connections produce happiness; abandonment from tribe generates stress—a scientific term known as *Bio-Psycho-Socio-Spiritual dysregulation.* Here's what this term means. When you experience any form of pain—biological, psychological, social, or spiritual—your Stone Age Tribe brain's built-in stress-response mechanism gets triggered irrespective of the catalyst for stress in your environment. *Pain—whether biological, psychological, social, or spiritual—is all the same to your brain.*

This state of pain takes you out of your equilibrium and puts your brain, body, and being into a dysregulated state of stress. Whenever your Stone-Age Tribe brain perceives a threat to your safety, security, and stability, your stress-response system activates. It doesn't matter if the stress is attributed to biological, psychological, social, or spiritual factors in your life, your stress mechanism activates in the same way.

Not only does abandonment from your tribe increase your risk of biological death, it threatens your psychological safety, your social stability, and your spiritual outlook on life. To your Stone-Age ancestors, a Happy Brain was simply survival—knowing you got to live another day. It's the reason why deeply imprinted into your Stone-Age Tribe brain, even today, is the belief why happiness equates to survival. Happiness in its primal form is about increasing the odds for life, which comes from being part of a tribe. What are the effects on your brain from feeling abandoned, isolated, or excluded from your tribe? It's not good news.

Your Despairing Brain

Again, your Stone-Age Tribe brain is fueled by the three important elements for ensuring survival—safety, security, stability— and it accomplished them by realizing the powerful advantage when you become part of a tribe. Human survival and your Happy Brain are intimately linked to tribe. While evolutionary psychology affirms banding into tribes continues to be a key strategy for human survival, brain science is shedding new insights how the absence of tribe poses a very heavy price on your health and happiness. A growing body of scientific evidence suggests the lack of tribe today is opening up the proverbial Pandora's box of discord and discontent, of angst and alienation. Why is this so dangerous? Abandonment from tribe— which manifests as the lack of community and the absence of in-person connection—is happening everywhere you look today. Do any of the following scenarios relate to you?

- Lack of dinnertime spent together means a loss of connection with your family.
- More screen-time on devices decreases your real-time interactions with others.
- The breakdown of the extended family leaves you feeling a lack of love and belonging.
- Fenced-in yards and gated communities cause fear in neighbors and raise social apathy.

There are likely more scenarios that come to mind. The increase in social isolation and physical alienation from others, witnessed in today's world, fuels your despairing brain. The more you suffer from a despairing brain, the more likely you are to succumb to the Disease of Despair rampant in society, witnessed as anger, anxiety, and addiction.

Findings recently presented at the 125th Annual Convention of the American Psychological Association in 2017 confirm how social isolation and feelings of loneliness—tangible products from the lack of tribe today—pose a grave detriment to your life. Julianne Holt-Lundstadt, a professor at Brigham Young University and the lead researcher of this study, poignantly warns, "Being connected to others socially is widely considered a fundamental human need— crucial to both well-being and survival...Yet an increasing portion of the U.S. population now experiences isolation regularly."[11] To put this in the most blunt way—without your tribe, you despair. Left unchecked, prolonged social isolation, resulting from lack of tribe in your life, accelerates the spread of the Disease of Despair.

What's even scarier is how the lack of tribe and the emotional loneliness it generates as the Disease of Despair can sabotage your ability for achieving balance, longevity, and resilience. Here's another example of how that occurs. A pioneering study on the link between physical isolation, social neglect, and mortality found that "people with stronger social relationships had a 50% increased likelihood of survival than those with weaker social relationships… These findings indicate that the influence of social relationships on the risk of death are comparable with well-established risk factors for mortality such as smoking and alcohol consumption and exceed the influence of other risk factors such as physical inactivity and obesity."[12]

But there exists a grave and pervasive issue society faces today. Further studies all point to a grim conclusion. Self-isolation, physical solitude, and emotional loneliness can attribute to premature death—posing an even greater risk for mortality than obesity, smoking, air pollution, and excessive alcohol consumption. Why should this be a wake-up call? These studies are a snapshot of how more segments of society are suffering from a despairing brain. What does that mean? In the United States nearly forty-three million Americans over the age of forty-five lament experiencing loneliness; a situation exacerbated with roughly 25 percent of Americans today living alone. In case there's any doubt, this is just one face of what suffering from a despairing brain looks like. A despairing brain is what happens when you lose the early human survival strategy to tribe.

It's important at this point to make a crucial distinction how social isolation isn't the same as the feeling of loneliness. The former is a physical state; the latter is an emotional state. There are many of you living on your own or being single—voluntarily or involuntarily—

[11.] Léo Surugue, "How loneliness and social isolation can kill more than obesity," *International Business Times*, Aug. 5, 2017.

[12.] Julianne Hold-Lundstadt et al., "Social Relationships and Mortality Risk: A Meta-analytic Review," Published: July 27, 2010.

who are healthy, well-adjusted folks who experience a deep sense of happiness and contentment in your life. There are also those of you living in major urban centers, who can be surrounded by millions of people, yet experience profound loneliness. Contrary to what society wants you to believe, money and wealth also don't guarantee your Happy Brain. I personally know and counsel individuals—who epitomize the societal criteria of success and fame—confessing to me their deep sense of despair and disillusionment in life.

Additionally, social isolation and the accompanying feelings of loneliness have no correlation to whether you consider yourself an introvert or an extrovert. It's fundamentally about your ability and capacity for nurturing healthy connections with others in life. Feeling lonely and being alone are not the same. I should know, as I myself at the time of writing this book live alone and consider myself to benefit from a Happy Brain.

There presently exists a tremendous peril to your happiness when you live in a society that literally disrupts the ancient wirings in your brain that evolved as a social organ. More people are going against what thousands of years of evolution sculpted your Social Brain to do—achieve safety, security, and stability derived from being part of a tribe. In a world that sees an increase in isolation, loneliness, and disconnection, your Social Brain morphs into a despairing brain that fuels society's collective anger, anxiety, and addiction.

Let's also not conflate your Social Brain with social media. Your Social Brain doesn't care so much about how many followers on Twitter or Instagram you have or how to maximize the number of people in your online social profile. The marvels of technology and social media are no substitute for what in-person, physical, real-time interactions bear for your Happy Brain. While screen-time and virtual reality are certainly cause for concern, society already finds many ways for you to starve your Social Brain from what it needs most for sustenance—attachment to tribe. What's being witnessed today is the negative side of the Happiness Equation where abandonment from tribe deprives your Social Brain from achieving happiness. It all can be summarized by the bottom half of the Happiness Equation:

Abandonment from Tribe = Death = Despairing Brain

Over the past few years, a primary focus in the training programs I deliver to the medical community and mental health professionals is the correlation between a despairing brain and the Disease of Despair. It's reassuring to observe that the medical community is gradually recognizing how the long-term damage produced by all aspects of stress—biological, psychological, social, and spiritual—exacerbates the epidemic of anger, anxiety, and addiction in the world.

Summarizing the main points from this lesson, your Social Brain is perhaps the most unsung hero of human evolution. Without your Social Brain, civilization might not have flourished, human language might not have developed, the ability to empathize or render trust might not have happened, humanity's most sacred rituals and religious traditions might not have manifested, and most importantly humans might not have become the dominant species on the planet today.

Here's one valuable take-away from this lesson. By learning to bond into social groups, your early ancestors increased their odds for survival. It's precisely this stark choice between life and death how early humans realized why solidifying into social groups—into tribes—increased not just your own, but everyone's odds for getting sustenance and shelter. Think about it this way. Humans aren't the fastest, strongest, nor largest species on the planet. But despite not having these prized attributes, there's one quality that you excel at more so than any other species—socialization. More precisely, humans mastered the ability for complex socialization. Banding into tribes promised the continuity of the human species.

The ability to tribe becomes the functional strategy behind your Social Brain. Cultivating tribe into your life nurtures your Social Brain and is the foundation for creating your Happy Brain. Yet the dangers currently faced in society are diminishing your ability to tribe and to thrive. The breakdown of strong communities, our adversarial political climate, the instilled fear of "the other," fixation on technology, and cultural discord appear to saturate your despairing brain. The lack of tribe in today's world fries the ancient wirings of your Social Brain. The result? Living in an age of amplified anger, anxiety, and addiction drives the Disease of Despair and hijacks your Happy Brain.

Humanity largely owes its success to the Social Brain. Yet society knows very little about its value and function, the power it has to promote your health and happiness; the potential it has to generate balance, longevity, and resilience; and the solution it now provides to create your Happy Brain. Having mastered this fundamental concept of your Social Brain and the Happiness Equation, you're now prepared for the next lesson.

Bonus Content

- Go to www.ScienceofaHappyBrain.com for exercises to promote your Social Brain.
- Watch video how your Social Brain operates and works.
- Discover exercises for building tribe in your own life.

LESSON FIVE

STOP HIJACKING YOUR HAPPINESS

> For every minute you are angry, you lose sixty seconds of happiness.
>
> —Ralph Waldo Emerson

The Four Happiness Hijacks

Congratulations, you've made it to the halfway point of your Happiness course. Before moving into the remaining lessons that focus on the four Happiness Strategies of your Happy Brain, it's important to recap some of the key points you've been learning in the previous lessons. Think of this lesson as the linchpin that summarizes the past four lessons, while introducing the next remaining ones that constitute the core of your Happiness course. This lesson explores the following:

1) How your Stone-Age Tribe brain perpetuates the four Happiness Hijacks that sabotage your Happy Brain.

2) How the four Happiness Strategies are established in the Bio-Psycho-Socio-Spiritual model of happiness and act as a solution for each Happiness Hijack.

3) How your Social Brain's drive for tribe is the basis behind the four Happiness Strategies and the secret for achieving your Happy Brain.

Let's start by exploring why operating out from your Stone-Age Tribe brain ultimately hijacks your chances for a Happy Brain and what you can do to put the brakes on it.

You've learned how your Stone-Age Tribe brain is exclusively focused on one thing—survival at all costs. It's what nature wants. Getting you to survive got you to reproduce to get more humans onto the world. In its most primal sense, the foundation of your Happy Brain is intimately linked with survival and your Stone-Age Tribe brain. There were two primary mechanisms evolution wired into your Stone-Age Tribe brain that became strategies for survival—avoiding pain and seeking pleasure. Pain can manifest as stress in your brain, body, and being. As you discovered, your brain evolved to make you process physical pain (biological) similarly to other forms of pain (psychological, social, or spiritual).

Because of your brain's built-in stress-response system, your brain is always looking out for threats in your environment that jeopardize your safety, security, and stability. As a result, your brain's negativity bias registers bad and painful experiences more strongly than good and pleasurable ones. Since your Stone-Age Tribe brain equates pain and stress as a threat to your survival, you've become programmed into believing you'll be happy if you only avoid and decrease all stress and pain from your life. This is the first Happiness Hijack: *Your Stone-Age Tribe brain dupes you into believing your Happy Brain comes from a life exclusively absent of strife, suffering, and stress.*

Nature is doubly cruel. Not only is your Stone-Age Tribe brain geared for avoiding pain, it's obsessed with maximizing pleasure. Evolution programmed your brain to release the neurotransmitter dopamine as a reward for accomplishing tasks that promote survival. Whether it's sex, food, sleep, or elimination, your Stone-Age Tribe brain motivates you to seek out and to repeat these experiences by perpetuating a state of dissatisfaction when the sensation of pleasure evaporates. It's a concept the Buddha understood as *duhkha*—you're never satisfied with what you have or with what is. This leads to the second Happiness Hijack: *Your Stone-Age Tribe brain's innate sense of dissatisfaction in the present moment and of anticipation over future rewards convinces you how maximizing pleasure is the key to your Happy Brain.*

Nature primed your brain to evolve for the avoidance of pain and the attachment to pleasure—both sabotages to your happiness. However, the one powerful advantage ancient humans possessed to combat the harshness of life in the Stone Age was the ability to create strong social bonds and communities for ensuring survival. Although early humans recognized how banding together into tribes was evolutionary advantageous, one of the biggest crises society faces today is the rise in physical isolation, emotional loneliness, and social disconnection. The common attitude prevalent today is the "go it alone" motto as the preferred way of life. Sadly, all of these issues accelerate the risk of illness, disease, and death. You now have the third Happiness Hijack: *Living in a society that promotes individualism and disconnection counters your Stone-Age Tribe brain's necessity for social solidarity that debilitates your Happy Brain.*

Although your Stone-Age Tribe brain is wired for survival, humans have the intrinsic capacity for altruism, empathy, and compassion toward members of their tribe. Unfortunately, there's a tendency not to impart empathy and act altruistically to those you consider to be "outside your tribe." It distorts the collaborative and communal benefits of tribe to the competitive and combative attributes of tribalism. The effects of tribalism—one directly negative consequence of your Stone-Age Tribe brain—are an impediment to your Happy Brain, as you can easily neglect the welfare and well-being of others you don't value as part of your tribe. This is the final Happiness Hijack: *Your Stone-Age Tribe brain's focus on the well-being for only those "in your tribe" creates a lack of empathy to those deemed "outside your tribe" that stunts everyone's Happy Brain by producing more anger, anxiety, and addiction in the world.*

What makes these four Happiness Hijacks so destructive is each one of them sabotages your personal capacity for achieving your Happy Brain—what I call a Personal Hijack. Second, they harm everyone else's Happy Brain by accelerating society's Disease of Despair—what I call a Popular Hijack that affects the greater population. Additionally, each of the four Happiness Hijacks sabotages one of the four corresponding Happiness Strategies. Here's a summary of the Four Happiness Hijacks and how they relate to what you've just learned.

Happiness Hijack No. 1—Happiness is merely the absence of pain.

a. Personal Hijack—Believing happiness comes from just avoiding pain sabotages your Happy Brain.

b. Popular Hijack—As a society, when we negatively define happiness by what it is not—the absence of pain—it fuels the Disease of Despair.

c. This hijacks the Biological Strategy for your Happy Brain.

Happiness Hijack No. 2—Happiness is the anticipation of future pleasure.

a. Personal Hijack—Your anticipation over future pleasure creates dissatisfaction in the present and sabotages your Happy Brain.

b. Popular Hijack—Society's fixation for seeking pleasure—manifesting as substance abuse, rampant consumerism, and digital dependency—fuels your suffering and the Disease of Despair.

c. This hijacks the Psychological Strategy for your Happy Brain.

Happiness Hijack No. 3—Happiness is an individual pursuit, not a collective one.

a. Personal Hijack—Leading a life lacking tribe and social connection adversely affects your health and sabotages your Happy Brain.

    b. Popular Hijack—Our cultural priority for individualism and independence fuels the rise of depression and suicide that manifests as the Disease of Despair.

    c. This hijacks the Social Strategy for your Happy Brain.

Hijack No. 4—Happiness is extending empathy to only those in your tribe.

    a. Personal Hijack—Limiting your compassion and altruism to only those you consider to be "in your tribe" sabotages your Happy Brain.

    b. Popular Hijack—Operating out of tribalism drives racism, enmity, and social injustice in the world and accelerates the Disease of Despair.

    c. This hijacks the Spiritual Strategy for your Happy Brain.

While these four Happiness Hijacks are personally detrimental to you, the worst part of all is how society can brainwash you into accepting each of these Happiness Hijacks as strategies for you to achieve a Happy Brain—when, in fact, they produce the opposite effect. Brain science is affirming how each of these Happiness Hijacks sabotages your Happy Brain, while also increasing the Disease of Despair. So why is this situation so dire? All four Happiness Hijacks are playing out in today's world and continue to become embedded into the current social narrative of happiness many have come to embrace as truths.

Why do I believe this? At various stages in my own life, I myself bought into each one of these social narratives of happiness as absolute truths. I came to realize—sometimes painfully—just how strongly these social constructs became my own Happiness Hijacks. Now as someone who investigates the link between the brain and human behavior, I'm able to understand the science that backs up why buying into these social narratives ultimately hijacks your happiness.

It's from my own travails and triumphs in life I can say with certainty why these four Happiness Hijacks need to be dispelled in order for you to experience a Happy Brain. Unfortunately, these Happiness Hijacks are ones that still remain the predominant cultural constructs of happiness that contemporary society programs you to believe. It's a concept in behavioral science known as a *cognitive bias*. Think of a cognitive bias as the "frame of reality," through which an individual or a social group views the world. As you'll discover in the remaining lessons, each of these four Happiness Hijacks is an expression of a cognitive bias that is a direct result of how the human brain evolved.

The cognitive biases that fuel these Happiness Hijacks are evolutionary relics of your Stone-Age Tribe brain. The Happiness Hijacks can be better understood in the context of your Stone-Age Tribe brain's quest for survival that evolutionary psychology and neurobiology attest. Endeavoring to eliminate these survival aspects of your Stone-Age Tribe brain would be like trying to get rid of your body's built-in respiratory system or stress response. You simply can't.

Just as studies now show how you can learn to regulate your breathing and control stress, discoveries in brain science advance how it's possible for you to regulate and to control these four Happiness Hijacks of human behavior that sabotage your Happy Brain. Although you never can completely eliminate these Happiness Hijacks from your life, every one of you has the power and potential to rein in these primal aspects of your human nature.

Recognizing how these Happiness Hijacks are aspects of your Stone-Age Tribe brain, which undermine your chances for achieving enduring happiness, is one primary feature advanced in your Happiness course. More importantly, I want you to acquire the applied strategies in order for these cognitive biases to stop hijacking your Happy Brain. In order to achieve that goal, it's necessary to understand how your brain evolved in the context of evolution and how human behavior simultaneously sabotages and supports happiness. Your Happy Brain isn't only possible, brain science affirms it's achievable. Let's introduce the four Strategies of your

Happy Brain and their relationship to the greater Bio-Psycho-Socio-Spiritual model.

The Four Strategies for Your Happy Brain

What follows is the foundation for the remaining lessons that details the four Happiness Strategies requisite for you to achieve a Happy Brain. If the four Happiness Hijacks are residuals from your primal Stone-Age Tribe brain, the four Happiness Strategies are the products of your more evolved Social Brain. The four Happiness Strategies directly relate to the potent Happiness Equation you've learned—the drive to be attached to a tribe is the source of your Happy Brain. Let's introduce each Happiness Strategy before you learn them in the subsequent lessons.

Biological Comfort—The Biological Strategy for Happiness derives from the *Comfort* you experience from belonging to a strong, supportive tribe. Knowing you have the comfort of your tribe during times of personal strife and communal crisis generates the safety net that allows you to regain feeling in control of your life. The Biological Strategy for Happiness is a feature of evolutionary neuropsychology that meets your primal drive for physical safety, security, and stability essential to pursue your dreams and aspirations in life. It's about learning to accept the support and security from your tribe to help you control the controllable. Comfort is the Biological Strategy for your Happy Brain that allows you to experience personal safety and to accept communal security from your tribe in a chaotic and confusing world. *Comfort is the Biological Strategy for Happiness in order for you to achieve a Happy Brain.*

Psychological Contribution—The Psychological Strategy for Happiness derives from feeling a sense of *Contribution* with what you do in life that benefits not just you, but benefits others—your tribe. Contribution focuses on more than just the blind pursuit of making *money*; contribution is what brings you *meaning*. The Psychological Strategy of Contribution is similar to what the world's spiritual traditions teach about the importance of finding your life's calling or abiding in your *dharma*. Contribution is the Psychological Strategy for your Happy Brain that meets your primary drive for feeling value, belonging, and engagement in the world. *Contribution is the Psychological Strategy for Happiness that actualizes your values and life's purpose for achieving a Happy Brain.*

Social Connection—The Social Strategy for Happiness that comes from enjoying a positive and nurturing *Connection* with loved ones, your community, and even with the environment empowers your Happy Brain. Research affirms how social bonding and pro-social behaviors are essential for human behavior. Connection is the Social Strategy for your Happy Brain that increases the aptitude to build trust, improve performance, and promote resilience in groups—in classrooms, communities, and in the corporate world. *Connection is the Social Strategy for Happiness that allows you to gain prosperity and abundance in life from being part of a tribe in order to generate a Happy Brain.*

Spiritual Compassion—The Spiritual Strategy for Happiness results from cultivating *Compassion* first for yourself, then to others in your tribe, and eventually extending it to those you tend to view as outside of your tribe. While tribe can act as a powerful force for good in the world, when it morphs into tribalism, it has the damaging potential to create social division and cultural discord. Compassion is the Spiritual Strategy for your Happy Brain taught by the world's religions and faiths, as expressed by the Golden Rule—treat others as you would like them to treat you. *Compassion is the Spiritual Strategy for Happiness that allows you to extend empathy and tolerance in the world that empowers you and others to enjoy a Happy Brain.*

A key outcome from your Happiness course is learning to practice regularly the four Happiness Strategies of Comfort, Contribution, Connection, and Compassion that become the basis for your Happy Brain. The four Happiness Strategies just outlined are aspects of your Social Brain. They act as an antidote for the corresponding Happiness Hijacks that are products of your Stone-Age Tribe brain. Here they are:

1) **COMFORT**
   a. Comfort is the Biological Strategy for your Happy Brain.
   b. The Happiness Strategy of Comfort resolves Happiness Hijack No. 1: Happiness is merely the absence of pain.

2) **CONTRIBUTION**
   a. Contribution is the Psychological Strategy for your Happy Brain.
   b. The Happiness Strategy of Contribution resolves Happiness Hijack No. 2: Happiness is the anticipation of future pleasure.

3) **CONNECTION**
   a. Connection is the Social Strategy for your Happy Brain.
   b. The Happiness Strategy of Connection resolves Happiness Hijack No. 3: Happiness is an individual pursuit, not a collective one.

4) **COMPASSION**
   a. Compassion is the Spiritual Strategy for your Happy Brain.
   b. The Happiness Strategy of Compassion resolves Happiness Hijack No. 4: Happiness is extending empathy and love only to those you know.

The following table reveals how the four Happiness Strategies, the four Happiness Hijacks, and the Bio-Psycho-Socio-Spiritual model all converge in order for you to experience a Happy Brain.

Table 2

HAPPINESS ELEMENT	HAPPINESS STRATEGY	HAPPINESS HIJACK	HAPPY BRAIN
BIOLOGICAL	COMFORT	HAPPINESS IS ABSENCE OF PAIN	HAPPINESS IS COMFORT FROM YOUR TRIBE
PSYCHO-LOGICAL	CONTRI-BUTION	HAPPINESS IS FUTURE PLEASURE	HAPPINESS IS CONTRIBUTION TO YOUR TRIBE
SOCIAL	CONNEC-TION	HAPPINESS IS AN INDIVIDUAL MATTER	HAPPINESS IS CONNECTION WITH YOUR TRIBE
SPIRITUAL	COMPASSION	HAPPINESS EXTENDS ONLY TO YOU AND YOUR TRIBE	HAPPINESS IS COMPASSION FOR THOSE OUTSIDE YOUR TRIBE

I'm confident you're now prepared to master the remaining lessons that detail the individual Happiness Strategies of Comfort, Contribution, Connection, and Compassion that create your Happy Brain. Let's make that happen.

Bonus Content

- Visit www.ScienceofaHappyBrain.com and take the test to see if the Happiness Hijacks are present in your own life.
- Read more how these Happiness Hijacks undermine both personal and societal happiness.

LESSON SIX

THE HAPPINESS STRATEGY OF COMFORT

> Cure sometimes, treat often, comfort always.
>
> —Hippocrates

Taking Comfort in Your Tribe

As you move into the second half of your Happiness course, this lesson begins an in-depth exploration into each of the four Happiness Strategies for your Happy Brain—Comfort, Contribution, Connection, and Compassion. The next four lessons reveal to you how these four Happiness Strategies relate to the four Happiness Hijacks, the Bio-Psycho-Socio-Spiritual model, and the brain science behind each of them. Let's start with the Biological Happiness Strategy of Comfort.

Here's a question to consider. What do taking Tylenol and taking comfort in your tribe have in common? They both are effective and proven strategies employed for you to cope with pain. More precisely, taking Tylenol and taking comfort in your tribe soothe your brain in pain. While the former tends to be the more popular and convenient one most folks employ to alleviate pain, the latter is the original strategy for controlling pain that nature wired into your Social Brain. It turns out, taking a pain reliever does more than lessen the pain from a broken bone, it appears to soothe the suffering from a broken heart and allay the turmoil of a troubled soul.

Additionally, there exists a primal pain-regulation system that evolved in your brain that's shown to be as effective for comforting pain as taking a pain-reliever. Even more astounding, this system is an aspect of your Social Brain that is linked to the Happiness Equation.

A 2009 study observed the same active ingredient found in the common pain-reliever Tylenol also dampens physical, emotional, and social pain.[13] The findings from this specific study further support a fundamental truth—you're a social being whose brain evolved to feel all forms of pain. As you recall, there exist shared neural networks and overlapping regions in your brain that experience and regulate all forms of pain—biological, psychological, social, and spiritual. Whether it's a headache or heartache, a broken bone or broken heart, you'll generally go to any means to comfort your pain.

Why I find the word *comfort* to be so appropriate as the Biological Strategy for your Happy Brain is the origin of the word itself. The English word *comfort* derives from the Old French *confort*, which in turn goes back to the Latin *confortare* "to console, to be strong together." It's this original essence of the word *comfort* that's used to imply anything that gives strength and fortitude to you in times of strife and struggle. It's what biology required and what the Social Brain wired into human behavior—taking comfort in your tribe helps you cope with life's hardships.

United by Grief

Sometimes the tribe in which you find yourself being in happens not by personal choice, but from tragic circumstance. Such is the case for my dear friend, Cara. She belongs to a unique community of people that no one voluntarily chooses to be in and one you can never leave. What is this tribe? Parents who endure the shared anguish from having lost a child.

[13.] "Could acetaminophen ease psychological pain?" *Science Daily*, Dec. 25, 2009.

Cara's permission to share her personal story exposed to me a powerful truth—grief cannot be viewed through a universal lens. The loss of a child is an expression of raw grief distinguished from the death of a parent, partner, or sibling. Although the anguish I feel from Mom's suicide is profound, Cara's grief results from having tragically lost both of her two sons as young adults in the span of three years, due to different circumstances. Her pain illuminates a form of suffering many of you hopefully will never have to face. Although you will experience the inevitable death of a loved one at some point in your life, the inconsolable grief that comes from the tragedy of a parent's losing a child—regardless if the death is anticipated or unexpected—is a form of suffering no one is ever fully prepared to bear.

My interview with Cara exposed how the aftermath from the death of a child does more than destroy the life of a parent, it shatters one's very identity. It questions one's sense of self-worth and breaks one's state of happiness. Here is Cara's personal experience that she volunteered to reveal in her own words:

> What you come to learn when you lose a child, or children, is that it's a unique kind of grief. We've both lost parents, we've both lost friends. But what makes it different is that being a parent is a key factor in one's identity. My identity isn't connected to my parents nor my friends, so more than anything, my sons' deaths decimated my identity. What I've found is that when anyone loses a loved person, we all gather around, we send condolences, we know what comforting things to say. But none of that works if you're a parent who loses a child. It's a unique experience that also never leaves you, because being a parent is who you are. There's also no consolation, compensation, even comfort. There's nowhere to go for those things. They can never fill the hole in your identity that has been shattered.

This tribe of parents bound by the death of a child is shaped by a specific form of grief I will never imagine nor pretend to know. While the daily level of struggle that Cara wakes up with never diminishes, her situation exemplifies a form of comfort that comes not from condolences nor the passage of time, but in knowing that she's not alone.

Comfort can manifest as shared empathy. Cara belongs to a tribe united by grief—a specific level of anguish only they know. Cara's despair links her to a community of people that transcends ideology, politics, gender, race, religion, sexuality, and socio-economic status. What unifies them is the special circumstance of their pain and the utter destruction of identity that a child's death generates. For Cara there exists comfort in the recognition that others in this tribe have mutual experiences, including a depth of suffering she endures. It's the shared identification over the pain from a parent's loss of a child that's the sacred bond uniting this tribe. To witness and commiserate over their common grief is the sole expression of comfort they feel capable to give and receive.

As Cara herself states, "The utter shattering of one's identity is the core of it. I've spoken with others in my position. I check in on them, even though we're not close geographically. But we've become a tight community. In fact, one of the sad things that happened to me is a woman I've recently known through my profession sent me an e-mail just before Thanksgiving to inform me her son just died. One of the lines I'll always remember from her message is: 'We have more in common now.' I know if she were to come here, we'd have such a level of connection."

It's the anguished sentiment expressed in the *TIME* article "United by Grief," in which Joe Samaha recounts the heartbreak from having tragically lost his 18-year-old daughter in the horrific 2007 Virginia Tech shooting. He reflects, "We understand the pain, the trauma and the long-term aftermath. It's a brother and sisterhood."[14] More than half of those interviewed for this piece

---

14. Haley Sweetland Edwards and Belinda Luscombe, "United by Grief: Parents who lose a child to a school shooting discover a bond that transcends ideology,"

described a permanent, profound loss of self after their child's death. "I used to have a good life, a blessed life, but it's ruined now,"[15] says Andrew Pollack. Samaha and Pollack convey what Cara knows to be true—only those who've lost a child will fully share her despair. It's a tenuous connection, but for those in this tribe the comfort required is merely to be seen, to be heard, and to know their pain is mutually felt. It's what your Social Brain demands. Cara views her situation by stating the following:

> I have more in common with the parents of sons and daughters killed in Iraq, the parents of sons and daughters killed in nightclub shootings, terrorist attacks, or anything like that. All those people, I'll never know them, but if we were to talk, we would all say the same thing: I can never get my happiness back. So, all the comfort you or anyone else can heap on me, really doesn't change that. I just have to work with it each day… Another thing happened after the word got out about my son's death. There were many professional colleagues who reached out with messages of sympathy. But what I couldn't have known is that there were people who reached out to me—many of whom I've known for years— and they shared with me that that they, too, had lost a child. Now I never would've known this. And those are the people who recognize me, and I recognize them.

How does Cara's experience relate to the Biological Strategy of Comfort? Whenever you experience grief or are overwhelmed with despair, what the human spirit requires most is simply for your pain and suffering to be recognized. As the author and Christian social

---

TIME Dec. 10, 2018, 30.
15. Ibid.

activist Parker Palmer rightfully declares, "The human soul doesn't want to be advised or fixed or saved. It simply wants to be witnessed—to be seen, heard and companioned exactly as it is."[16]

Yet, there's an instinctive human tendency "to fix the problem" or "to save the person" in pain. It's actually a biological drive of the human species and a function of your Social Brain—you just hate seeing those you love unduly suffering. Despite coming from the best of intentions, your desire to console those in despair often stems from self-interest, just as much as genuine intent. Perhaps as a survival strategy and way to alleviate your own discomfort, your Social Brain incentivizes you to allay those in your tribe to be free from pain and anguish. In actuality, the most valuable action you can take when comforting another in despair is not to advise them, but to acknowledge them. The next time those you know are afflicted by grief, let them know you simply care and just be a compassionate witness to their pain. It's such a simple act that brings tremendous comfort.

Cara's personal tragedy underscores an important point for you in this lesson—there are tribes in your life that extend beyond blood ties and friends. I don't assume parents who lose a child will ever achieve a state of happiness they once enjoyed. What I claim is how Cara is now part of a tribe that recognizes her pain—something that no one else in her immediate circle will know. In this way, comfort comes in knowing that your anguish is witnessed and heard from those in your tribe. The Biological Strategy of Comfort is remembering you're not alone.

What is pain? How do humans employ language to describe it? Here's something I want you to consider. Have you ever stopped to think how you use language to talk about pain? Have you ever said or heard anyone say the following phrases: "My heart got hurt really bad after she left me," "My hopes feel broken," "His ego got bruised," or "Why is my soul in so much pain?" Such phrases exist not just in English but also in countless languages across the world.

---

16. Parker Palmer, "The Gift of Presence, the Perils of Advice," *On Being*, Apr. 27, 2016.

Of course, these phrases are more figurative compared to when you say, "I broke my right femur," "He tore his ligament," or "I burst a blood vessel." It's the reason why you use the same verbs such as "hurt, ache, bruise, crush, burst, and break" to describe both physical and non-physical pain. The phenomenon for employing the same words to express physical and non-physical pain is a universal feature of human language. Pain is all the same to your brain.

As noted social neuroscientist Matthew Lieberman aptly suggests, "We distinguish various kinds of pain, and social pain ought to be awarded membership in the pain club."[17] Although you experience the gamut of pain—not just physical, you can still process it as biological pain. It doesn't matter if you speak English, Korean, Arabic, or Dutch, every one of you communicates in the same way when you experience pain. As I like to say, "Everyone laughs and laments in the same language."

While language affirms this point, there's a common tendency in society to conceptualize non-physical forms of pain—such as emotional or psychological pain—metaphorically, rather than literally. Here's an example. When you hear the phrase "I'm suffering from a broken heart," there's often a habit to regard the pain figuratively as a metaphor, rather than a reality of an actual physically ruptured heart. This metaphorical usage of pain in speech often leads to a cognitive bias suggesting how all forms of non-physical pain, that is psychological, social, or spiritual, are less valid—less felt—than the physical sensation of pain. Yet, if you've ever grieved from the loss of a loved one, experienced agony from a brutal break-up, or felt betrayed by a trusted friend, you know just how viscerally that pain actually feels biologically in your body. Non-physical pain might not be tangible or localized to a specific area of your body, but emotional pain hurts; social pain is real.

To help you understand just how powerful non-physical pain is, let me show you by engaging you in another exercise. If you feel it's okay, I wish for you to recall one of the most difficult and challenging

---

[17] Matthew Lieberman, "The social brain and its superpowers," *TEDx St. Louis*, Oct. 7, 2013.

moments of your life. If it feels comfortable and safe for you, take a minute and allow the memory of this specific painful event to be felt in your body. Having done so, what was the memory that you recalled? For most of you, I bet it was unlikely the memory of an actual physical pain, but rather a situation when you experienced psychological, social, or spiritual pain. Maybe it was the painful memory of losing a family member, a beloved pet, or possibly ending a special relationship. Were you able to feel in your body the emotional pain linked with that memory?

Okay. Now, if I were to ask you to recall the memory of a time when you endured intense physical pain—breaking a bone, getting injured playing sports, squirming through painful dental work, or recovering from surgery—I bet most of you would be able to recount the circumstances around the event itself. Now let's try something else. I'd like to ask if you're able to bring up the actual severity from that pain in your body you experienced at the time. That is, can you literally re-feel the physical pain from that time as you remember the event? Are you able to re-experience the actual physical pain from that event?

I'd wager the majority of you could summon up the pain relived from a distressing emotional event in your life, but very few of you could do the same from remembering the pain in your body generated from physical pain. Do you wonder why that is?

Unless your physical pain is chronic or unabated—let's say from fibromyalgia, rheumatoid arthritis, or from a permanent physical disability—the sensation of physical pain tends to be temporary and eventually fades. But pain that's a result from social, emotional, spiritual, or psychological trauma is another matter. Those forms of pain generally endure and register more strongly in your brain, body, and being. Specifically, your amygdala and hippocampus—regions of your brain's limbic system—collectively govern the link between emotional stimuli and long-term memory. In the exercise I just had you perform, your recollection from an experience that produced non-physical pain is more prone to be wired firmly into your long-term memory than physical pain. Why would this be the case? What would be the rationale for your brain to hold onto more strongly and your body to remember more readily emotional, psychological, and social pain versus physical pain?

The answer resides again in the ancient past that reverts to the primal Happiness Equation of your Social Brain where attachment to tribe is life; abandonment from tribe is death. A possible reason why psychological, social, and spiritual pain is felt more potently than physical or biological pain is that social affliction became far more crucial for survival of the species than biological damage to your individual body. Here's an even simpler explanation—your body has its own autonomic ability to mend a broken bone and heal from a cut. Given enough time and rest, your broken bone will repair itself; your cut will soon mend. Your body's biology will naturally heal and self-regulate.

A social wound, psychological blow, or emotional scar, however, is an entirely different matter. Whatever way social pain is caused— by rejection or by abandonment from others—your body cannot cure these wounds naturally in the same way as a physical bruise. Your body doesn't have an innate biological ability to mend your broken heart, as it readily does your broken bone. This is precisely why the emotional trauma you feel from the death of a loved one takes much longer to heal than physical distress to your body.

While biology made it possible for your body to repair itself physically, evolution did create a powerful remedy for you to heal from psychological, social, and spiritual pain—the Happiness Strategy of Comfort. Taking comfort in your tribe is the Biological Strategy for your Happy Brain. While it's true taking Tylenol can temporarily dull the biological pain from a headache or heartache, the enduring and most curative strategy for healing pain—especially psychological, social, and spiritual—is social solidarity. *Your Social Brain's tactic for regulating pain from seeking support from your tribe is the Biological Happiness Strategy of Comfort.*

Please Stop My Pain

One of the strongest and enduring forms of pain you can feel is the distress your Social Brain experiences as the result of social abandonment, physical neglect, and emotional loss. The pronounced pain experienced in your brain, body, and being when separated from those you're emotionally, psychologically, and socially bonded to—your tribe—is witnessed not just in humans, but also in other mammals. It's a phenomenon of your Social Brain that neurobiology and evolutionary psychology refer to as *separation distress* or *separation anxiety disorder*. Why are these important terms to know? Both separation distress and separation anxiety disorder happen to be the factors precipitating society's Disease of Despair that sabotage your Happy Brain.

Separation distress and separation anxiety disorder manifest in numerous ways. There are of course the usual ways that come to mind, such as a child getting lost in a busy airport, unexpectedly getting fired from a job of many years, ending a marriage or a long-term relationship, or the death of a loved one. But there recently exists equally damaging ways that society produces the trauma endured in your Social Brain.

As you learned from previous lessons, in the absence of tribe, your Social Brain despairs. We've become a society gradually dying on the inside for we've lost the powerful bond of belonging to a modern-day tribe. The loss of tribe in our twenty-first century technologically advanced culture—which, in case you need to be reminded, isn't in your cyber-tribe—leads to an endemic of emptiness, causing unrelenting pain and irreparable damage to our collective health, economy, and society. In whichever way you experience separation distress, the result is the same—pain. But there's good news.

There exists a marvelous system wired into your brain that evolved to regulate pain—your brain's opioid system. This system exists as your brain's built-in coping mechanism that serves the purpose to control pain in whatever form it manifests in your life. Let's investigate what exactly your brain's opioid system does, how it interacts with your Social Brain, and how it reflects as the Biological Happiness Strategy of Comfort.

You already learned of the convincing evidence that supports how your brain evolved a strategy for survival—by developing neural structures that allow you to process social pain as if it were physical pain. That's the *why*, but the other question is *how*. The answer now appears to be an important system wired into your brain that regulates pain—the opioid system. Again, as renowned social neuroscientist Lieberman indicates, "Social attachments functioned by piggybacking onto the physical pain system and did so through the opioid process. Opioids are the brain's natural painkillers. Their production and release diminish the experience of pain."[18] The idea behind how your brain developed a mechanism to release opioids in order to soothe the pain of separation distress is known as the *Brain's Opioid Theory of Social Attachment (BOTSA)*.

Unless you're an avowed masochist, you generally avoid pain at all cost. It's a core principle expressed throughout evolutionary biology, psychology, and sociology. BOTSA is nature's strategy that allows for you to regulate the pain produced by separation distress by mimicking it as physical pain in your brain. It now makes sense why the opioid system is the same mechanism that simultaneously regulates both social pain and physical pain.

Any organism in pain—whether it's a single-cell amoeba, you, or society—will respond in the same manner when trying to regulate pain, irrespective if it's biological, psychological, social, or spiritual. You'll go to any means possible to minimize your pain. It's this very reason why your brain developed a natural strategy to cope with and to control social pain. It's your brain's opioid system that encourages you to seek out social attachment from pain felt in times of crisis and conflict.

According to this theory, "BOTSA predicts that social isolation results in low levels of endogenous opioids, motivating the individual to seek social contact. Social contact duly results in the release of endogenous opioids, consummatory reward and an associated feeling

---

18. Lieberman, *Social*, 49.

of euphoria and contentment."[19] So how does this scientific study directly apply to you? For early humans, the power to tribe is far more than a mere survival strategy for staying alive; it becomes a potent way for your Social Brain to respond to and control pain. BOTSA—the Brain's Opioid Theory of Social Attachment—is the neural mechanism behind the Biological Happiness Strategy of Comfort. *To socialize is to survive, but to socialize is also to soothe.*

The way BOTSA regulates pain is how your Social Brain allows you to experience the Biological Happiness Strategy of Comfort. Before the discovery and usage of alcohol, drugs, natural herbs, and pharmaceuticals by humans, your brain's natural opioid system favored the power of social attachment and the drive for belonging to a tribe as the preferred and most trusted analgesic. Think of your tribe as nature's original Tylenol. That has all changed in today's world, where there are several non-natural ways—by this I mean coping strategies that aren't an organic product of human evolution and your Social Brain—you hope will mimic BOTSA and release endorphins to alleviate your pain.

In a time when the absence of tribe fuels disconnection and the Disease of Despair, your Social Brain goes malnourished. Society's Disease of Despair is the product from an explosion of social pain amidst society. Senior citizens living alone, technology at the dinner table, isolated cubicles in office spaces, and gated suburban communities are just some of the tangible manifestations that attribute to an increase in society's Disease of Despair.

The demise of tribe deprives you from your natural ability of the brain's opioid system to help control and regulate pain when it manifests in your life. It's BOTSA that empowered early humans to cope with the harshness of a world rife with conflict and chaos. This concept of BOTSA is best summed up by a traditional saying I often hear from my Indian relatives: "Joy when shared is doubled. Misery when shared is halved." You instinctively turn to others in both good

---

[19] A. J. Machin and R. Dunbar, "The brain's opioid theory of social attachment: A review of the evidence," Behaviour 55 148(9-10):985-1025, Sept. 2011.

times and bad to share your sadness and elation. It's what your Social Brain demands—taking comfort in your tribe.

Most of you know this to be true. How many of you have ever instinctively called someone you trust or ran into the arms of someone you love upon hearing or experiencing bad news? If you've ever done so, you can thank your Brain's Opioid Theory of Social Attachment (BOTSA) for making that possible. You can better understand the Biological Happiness Strategy of Comfort in the context of your Social Brain and this variation of the Happiness Equation:

Attachment to Tribe = Comfort = Happy Brain
Abandonment from Tribe = Discomfort = Despairing Brain

In the absence of tribe, your brain's opioid system becomes disrupted. Living in a society that fosters separation distress and separation anxiety disorder—from not having your tribe to turn to—jeopardizes the capacity for balance, longevity, and resilience in your life. In the absence of tribe, your Social Brain is forced to regulate the pain from a despairing brain in artificial ways, such as through recreational drugs, alcohol, prescription painkillers, and behaviors that mimic your brain's natural release of opioids—like checking your smartphone every five minutes. Guess what, you now have one potent cause for addiction. You also have an explanation for why those who experience trauma and PTSD can turn to substance abuse, as a coping mechanism, when the necessary social support systems are lacking in their life. It's the tragic condition of PTSD witnessed in many returning combat veterans or children who've endured abuse or trauma. While drugs and medication are certainly effective means for treatment, they require something more fundamental. Those suffering from PTSD need to feel part of a tribe that provides them the Biological Comfort required for healing their traumatized Social Brain.

In whichever way you experience the distress from social separation, neglect, or isolation, your Social Brain becomes scrambled and can make you feel hopeless and lost. Think of your entire Social Brain system as nature's form of "social insurance" that guarantees your need for social contact and attachment to your tribe. Comfort—in the form of seeking out others in your tribe—becomes evolution's Biological Strategy for your Happy Brain.

Biologists agree nature allowed for your brain, body, and being to evolve for survival. Evolution is efficient, as it has only one goal in mind—survival of the species. It's why opposable thumbs for grasping tools, vocal cords for speech, and the brain's opioid system for regulating pain all are part of your human anatomy today; they're all strategic traits that favor survival. The brain's opioid system and BOTSA are essentially your pain regulatory system whose motto continues to be *less pain enhances survival*.

Biological Comfort is one powerful tactic that creates your Happy Brain. Creature comforts, such as worldly possessions and riches, can never truly substitute your Social Brain's primal biological drive for seeking safety and knowing you're deeply cared for by others.

It's precisely what Dr. Deepak Chopra and Dr. Rudy Tanzi outline in *Super Brain* when they discuss the seven factors for an optimal brain: "(1) Sleep time, (2) physical time, (3) focus time, (4) time in, (5) down time, (6) play time, and (7) connecting time."[20] Don't get me wrong. I know many of you properly engage in activities to nourish your brain with the right food, the power of meditation, the benefits of exercise, and sufficient sleep. What's often neglected or overlooked when it comes to experiencing your Happy Brain, is the last point outlined by Chopra and Tanzi—connecting time.

As the authors go on to state: "No separate region of the brain oversees the merging of these [seven] needs to make a fully developed person. It takes the entire brain acting as an integrated whole. Happiness is then rooted in the feeling that you are complete."[21] What makes you complete, what makes you happy? what makes you healthy It's knowing you have others in your life who love and care for you. Your Happy Brain is nourished by the comfort you get from being part of a tribe. *Biological Comfort is what early humans discovered*

20. Deepak Chopra and Rudolph Tanzi, *Super Brain: Unleashing the Explosive Power of Your Mind to Maximize Health, Happiness, and Spiritual Well-Being* (Three River Press, New York: 2012), 188.

21. Ibid., 187.

would ensure the tribe to thrive that now becomes the foundation for your Happy Brain.

Comfort Creates Your Happy Brain

Many are left largely uninformed and unaware by the dangers from an atrophied Social Brain. The diminishment of tribe in today's world—reflected by lack of community, social disconnection, and emotional disengagement from others—yields society's Disease of Despair. The result? You experience real biological pain in your brain. This situation relates to the first Happiness Hijack: *Happiness is merely the absence of pain.*

In the training programs I provide for mental and behavioral health organizations, I advocate how the alarming opioid epidemic faced today cannot simply be remedied by just prescribing alternative forms of medication. I agree this measure absolutely needs to be part of an integrative strategy. Yet, the crucial element often overlooked when addressing the addiction epidemic is the pain experienced in your Social Brain in an age when so many suffer from social isolation and emotional loneliness that lacking tribe brings. Your tribe extends beyond just family members. Your tribe are those people in your life that you turn to for support and sustenance. It's the very reason why organizations such as Alcoholics Anonymous or support groups are so therapeutic and effective in treating addiction—belonging to a supportive community heals the trauma of your despairing brain.

Biological Comfort that manifests as the timeless therapy of tribe is what counters this first Happiness Hijack. When the social glue that binds the tribe together dissolves and the Disease of Despair ensues, your Social Brain has limited options available in order to cope with the insurmountable pain of social stress and the feelings of loneliness. If the pain caused by separation distress—from social isolation or from losing your sense of belonging to a tribe—is so prolonged, goes unrecognized, or when all hope for comfort feels lost, the tragic outcome is the Disease of Despair.

Living during a time when the necessity for tribe is devalued, it gradually leaves your Social Brain undernourished. It's likely a leading factor over the past few decades for the breakdown in social well-being, the underlying issue of our emotional poverty, and the fraying of the social fabric happening all around us. All of which result in more people experiencing greater depression, anxiety, addiction, trauma, and stress. These are all symptoms of society's Disease of Despair.

What's often the primary method to treat the mental, behavioral, and psychological disorders that result from the Disease of Despair? We do it through medication, counselling, therapy, and behavioral modification. While I don't dispute all these treatments have tremendous value and are certainly effective, they fail to address the core underlying symptom—a dysregulated Social Brain that craves connection and belonging. The Social Brain's Biological Strategy of Comfort is your reminder that evolution already created a neurobiological means for you to regulate and manage pain— socialization and attachment to your tribe trigger the brain's opioid system. Biological Comfort manifests by learning to turn to your tribe in times of strife and struggle.

Biological Comfort brings balance, longevity, and resilience into your life. It accomplishes this by allowing you to tap into the most potent form of medicine nature wired into your brain—the power of tribe. With regard to resilience, learning how to bounce back from adversity in life during times of hardship is a life-skill everyone needs to acquire. It's actually a key outcome of your Happiness course that I earnestly want you to implement into your life. Knowing you have the security and safety of people you can turn to for comfort in moments of anguish and angst is one reason why your brain evolved to become a Social Brain. Resilience is one product of your Happy Brain that comes from advancing Biological Comfort in the form of seeking solace in your tribe.

Comfort intimately relates to your Social Brain in a profound way that's best expressed by an Irish proverb a friend once told me. In Ireland, when someone experiences the loss of a loved one, instead of the traditional expression of condolences "I'm very sorry for your loss," the Irish say, "I'm here for you." The simplicity and authenticity of this Irish phrase embodies humanity's Biological Strategy of Comfort that you get from tribe. Comfort is the Biological Strategy for your Happy Brain generated from knowing that you're protected, nurtured, and supported by your tribe. *Experiencing Biological Comfort on a regular basis from attachment to your tribe strengthens your Happy Brain.*

It's the very same life-lesson I learned on the day and during the weeks after Mom's suicide. In my time of deepest need, my tribe came to my rescue. After Mom's tragic and unexpected suicide, I came to realize it was precisely the power of tribe that allowed me to embark on my own healing journey and ultimately empowered me to claim my Happy Brain. It was Biological Comfort that undeniably helped me get through a time when I felt spiritually impoverished and emotionally deplete. Here's how I discovered the real meaning of my Happy Brain and the value of my tribe.

After receiving that fateful call from Dad and his message— "Mom's in a coma at the hospital. You need to come home right away!"—in a state of complete and utter shock and denial, I was at a loss for what to do. Living on my own at the time, there was only one thing I wanted more than anything—the social support and comfort of others. Primed by thousands of years of evolution, my Social Brain instinctively kicked into overdrive.

I summed up the will to phone one of my closest friends, Steve, who drove thirty minutes from his place in Santa Monica to my apartment near UCLA. It was Steve who was on the phone with the airline and booked me on the first flight out the next morning from Los Angeles to my family home in Chicago. Knowing how upset and distraught I was, Steve even helped me pack my bag, drove me to his place, and let me stay in his guest room that night so I wouldn't be alone. It was Steve who drove me to the airport early morning and made sure I got on my flight. Steve's presence and patience during what I would unarguably call the most tragic night of my life is a testament to the power of tribe. From booking my airline ticket, helping me pack, letting me stay in his guest room, to getting me on the plane, Steve provided me something that was most valuable to me during that time of crisis—*Biological Comfort that comes from being part of a tribe.*

Happy Brain Homework

As part of your Happiness course, I encourage you to participate in various exercises that are backed up by brain science research and derive from universal spiritual wisdom for you to achieve the benefits of a Happy Brain. Your first homework is the "Gratitude and Recognition" task. In this exercise I ask for you to bring to mind at least one person who made or currently makes it possible for you to go about your day with more ease. It can even be someone from your past who has provided your present life with a greater sense of comfort. The catch, it has to be a person you never before thought was relevant or have thanked in person. It can be someone you personally know, like your former high-school teacher who wrote a recommendation for you to attend college or maybe a former boss who helped launch your career. It can even be a person you indirectly know or with whom you have minimum social interaction, like the staff who cleans your college dormitory or office every day, or the security guard who keeps your building safe for you and your family.

Whether it's a former high school teacher who motivated you to succeed or the pharmacist who provides you with the regular medication for your kid to stay healthy, there are likely hundreds of unrecognized people you never think about who make your life both comfortable and enjoyable. The next step is for you to recognize and express gratitude to that person. Whether it's with a phone call, text, e-mail, or written letter to someone you personally know or merely saying "thank you" the next time you encounter that person you see regularly, I guarantee it will not only boost your own Happy Brain, but their Happy Brain. I invite you to do this exercise at some point this week. See how it makes you feel. Most of all, have fun with it!

The goal of this exercise is to raise awareness and make you more cognizant of the vast number of people—your larger tribe— who fulfill so many of your basic needs and create the foundation for your Biological Comfort in order for you to thrive in life. While it was abundantly clear thousands of years ago how vital tribe was for basic human survival, the same extent of value that tribe has in your life tends to be lost today.

This "Gratitude and Recognition" exercise is an opportunity that ultimately reveals to you the powerful role Biological Comfort manifests in your life. In addition to your benefitting from your immediate tribe—family and friends—in times of strife and crisis, there exists a larger tribe of people who are there to ensure your basic biological survival needs of sustenance, safety, and security get met daily.

This interconnected and vast network of people in your life—whether you know them by name or not—constitutes your tribe and to some extent assists you in generating Biological Comfort. Knowing that your tribe provides a structure for you to go about your day free from threats to survival promotes your Happy Brain.

Bonus Content

- Visit www.ScienceofaHappyBrain.com and begin to apply the Happiness Strategy of Comfort into your own life in order to enjoy the benefits of your Happy Brain.
- Explore more about the brain science behind "gratitude" and watch our video.
- Share your experience about how you felt from doing your "Gratitude and Recognition" exercise and invite others you know to participate in this task.

LESSON SEVEN

THE HAPPINESS STRATEGY OF CONTRIBUTION

If one lights a fire for others, it will also
brighten one's own way.
—Nichiren (Japanese Buddhist teacher)

Your Need to Feel Needed

In 2017, my research assistant, Caitlin, spoke to me about a young man she knew named Drake, whose life story she thought would be an ideal case study for my research. I requested an introduction to speak and interview Drake. Here's one of the first things Drake revealed to me in our talk: "I haven't shot anybody and killed them. But I've been involved in a very decent amount of violence. It's brutal violence. I can tell you countless stories of times that I've put people in the hospital. There was one specific time in 2009 when I was hit in the head with a baseball bat, like, twenty times." What made Drake experience and partake in such brutality?

At the young age of fourteen, Drake joined one of the country's notorious and most violent street gangs, the Crips. His decision to join the Crips was due to something so essential for life and your Social Brain—the need to feel needed. I want to share with you Drake's real-life story, as I feel it accurately reflects the Psychological Strategy of Contribution. Here's Drake in his own words:

I grew up in a regular home in Colorado, born into a family with loving parents and a little brother. I was just another regular white kid from the suburbs. But when my parents got divorced, I decided to stay and live in Colorado with my father. I didn't have any friends. No friends. When they split up, my only friend, my little brother, was moved to Cali to live with my mom. Dad worked nights and slept all day. I was free to go where I wanted. I met one person, who had lots of people around him, and because of that, I decided these were the people I was going to spend my life with. That dude was a gang member. That's why I joined the Crips. I finally found people who made me feel special.

Drake is describing the consequences of what it was like to grow up the entirety of his adolescence with the damages endured from a despairing brain. Drake was yet another victim to society's Disease of Despair. His Social Brain went years malnourished from being deprived of attachment with his most valuable tribe—his family. Despite millennia of human civilization and technological progress, you fundamentally remain a social creature, whose Social Brain is driven by three primary needs: (1) the need for *value*, (2) the need for *belonging*, and (3) the need for *engagement*.

This fundamental notion for feeling *value, belonging,* and *engagement* with your tribe is a powerful sentiment expressed in Sebastian Junger's popular book *Tribe*. As Junger affirms, "Humans don't mind hardship, in fact they thrive on it; what they mind is not feeling necessary. Modern society has perfected the art of making people not feel necessary."[22] The pain experienced from being deemed unnecessary is an anathema for your Social Brain and compromises your Happy Brain. When any of the three primary human drives

---

22. Sebastian Junger, *Tribe: On Homecoming and Belonging* (Twelve Publisher, 1st Edition, 2016), xvii.

of value, belonging, and engagement goes unmet, your Social Brain panics, causing you and society to spiral into crisis and chaos, triggering the Disease of Despair. When the lack of feeling a sense of value, belonging, and engagement is unrelenting, it triggers a cycle of despair and hopelessness that has the potential to accelerate the levels of anger, anxiety, and addiction in society.

In my role as a university educator, committed to the success and welfare of the next generation, I'm truly alarmed at the spike in depression, anxiety, and suicide rates among teens and young adults over the past few years. Furthermore, there's a disturbing trend many of my colleagues and I witness happening in high schools and college campuses across the nation. More youth today feel lost and hopeless, desperately yearning to discover meaning and purpose in an unpredictable and uncertain world. They're no longer exploring the existential question: "How should I live?" Instead, I'm anguished how many university students are struggling with a much more pressing and painful dilemma: "Why should I live?" If nothing else, this looming mental health crisis justifies the demand for offering this Happiness course and drives my mission as an educator.

Relating it to Drake, this is precisely the situation that he found himself in during his teenage years—a life of anger, anxiety, and addiction from years of social abandonment and emotional neglect, as a result of not feeling needed and necessary in his world. Drake desperately sought a reason to live and to know his life had meaning and value. It's likely one predominant factor what propels Drake—along with thousands of other boys and young men like him around the world—who feel the inextricable urge to seek out the social solidarity found within conforming tribes like street gangs or militant organizations. From the lens of the Social Brain model of human behavior, what these young men desperately yearn for is the primal need to feel needed. *What they lack and desire most is the Psychological Contribution that constitutes a Happy Brain.*

Why is Psychological Contribution required for achieving your Happy Brain? To answer that question, it's important to understand what exactly contribution is. Contribution is linked to the important factor of knowing others need you and your presence in the world—to your tribe—matters and is meaningful. The Dalai Lama expands on this core human value of feeling necessary in wisdom from Buddhist philosophy that underscores the human need for Psychological Contribution. He imparts below:

> Many are confused and frightened to see anger and frustration sweeping like wildfire across societies that enjoy historic safety and prosperity. But their refusal to be content with physical and material security actually reveals something beautiful: a universal human hunger to be *needed*. Being 'needed' does not entail selfish pride or unhealthy attachment to the worldly esteem of others. Rather, it consists of a natural human hunger to serve our fellow men and women.[23]

The wisdom the Dalai Lama refers to reflects humanity's and your essential requirement for Psychological Contribution. The reason Drake joined the Crips gang as a young teenager and stayed with them for seven years was to fulfill his Social Brain's drive to feel needed. Despite being distorted and destructive, it was the coping mechanism his malnourished Social Brain critically craved. The Crips gang was the vital antidote for his despairing brain that granted Drake his primal need to feel value, belonging, and engagement.

What was Drake's justification to join the Crips? His developing adolescent Social Brain yearned to be part of a tribe. Drake was convinced he found a tribe that permitted him to feel necessary; one that gave him a sense of purpose and meaning. To reiterate Drake's own words: "I finally found people who made me feel special." While Drake was longing for happiness and the urge to feel needed, what he was actually seeking was a sense of stability. Let's explore the brain science that explains the primal drive for stability in the context of evolution and your stress-response system.

[23.] The Dalai Lama and Arthur C. Brooks, "Dalai Lama: Behind Our Anxiety, the Fear of Being Unneeded," *New York Times Op-Ed*, Nov. 4, 2016.

Stress: You Just Can't Live Without It

You've already learned from a previous lesson a core feature across biology—the instinct for any living system to avoid pain. That's true whether that system is a cell, your body, an ant colony, or even a complex macro-organism such as a tribe. All of these systems are equally governed by a fundamental concept in biology known as *homeostasis*. The concept of homeostasis is one of the basic principles in the life sciences.

It essentially describes the biological process of self-regulation by an organism in response to environmental conditions that take it out of equilibrium, such as discomfort and pain. Homeostasis is the ability for any living system to return to its normal functionality and experience optimal orderliness. Homeostasis can also be viewed in the Bio-Psycho-Socio-Spiritual model of health. Here are examples of how homeostasis happens in your everyday life.

When your cells are invaded by a foreign pathogen—like the flu virus or allergens in the air—your body will produce white blood cells to counter the *biological* intruder. After weeks of intense mental focus working on a crucial project for an important client at work, your mind will naturally seek out *psychological* ways to restore calm and tranquility. Moving away from home for the first time to start college, once back over vacation you crave the *social* nourishment from being together with your family. When coping with the grief accompanied from a death in the family, you instinctively reach out to your loved ones for *spiritual* solace. Homeostasis can be framed as a Bio-Psycho-Socio-Spiritual strategy for an organism to achieve stability. Here's another equation that hopefully helps you to understand these concepts.

Attachment to Tribe = Homeostasis/Balance = Happy Brain
Abandonment from Tribe = Lack of Homeostasis/
Imbalance = Despairing Brain

As much as you seek stability and consistency, one of the biggest threats to homeostasis is stress. From the perspective of neurobiology, stress is the result from the activation of your body's *Hypothalamic Pituitary Adrenocortical axis* (HPA-axis) and the *Autonomic Nervous System* (ANS). In turn, both of these systems are coordinated by your brain's amygdala—a small region of cells located deep within the primal layer of your Stone-Age Tribe brain that regulates your response to fear, anger, sexual arousal, and aggression. You actually know the HPA-axis and ANS better as your "fight-flight-or-freeze" response that sends hormones such as cortisol and adrenaline—among others—into your bloodstream when you're exposed to threats in your environment. Collectively, they constitute a complex, integrated system that links together your nervous, endocrine, and immune system. In the context of your Social Brain, any form of social deprivation, separation distress, or abandonment from others—from your tribe—triggers your primal HPA-axis and ANS, which you then experience as stress.

Stress is essentially a product of *Bio-Psycho-Socio-Spiritual dysregulation*, as it disrupts homeostasis. Threats in your life can be physical or biological, such as avoiding a head-on car crash or a virus attacking your immune system; emotional or psychological, like panicking about an upcoming exam or not having money for both groceries and rent; social or spiritual, when experiencing a profound sense of isolation from others or feeling a lack of meaning in life. Of course, the triggers for stress can overlap various domains.

You really can't bad-mouth stress entirely, for there's a clear upside to its function in life. It's important to remember how stress played a vital role in human evolution and in the ability for the human race to survive. While stress in itself isn't the main sabotage to your Happy Brain, the danger occurs when you lack the coping mechanisms or the cognitive skills to regulate the biological, psychological, social, and spiritual dimensions of stress in your life.

In the case of Drake, the stress he endured from the absence of stability in his childhood, due to his family's split, manifested as Bio-Psycho-Socio-Spiritual dysregulation. It's the Bio-Psycho-Socio-Spiritual model of homeostasis that provides one plausible explanation for Drake to seek the stability he desperately craved. After the stress caused from his family's rupture—the only tribe he ever knew—Drake's developing adolescent Social Brain was willing to find attachment to any tribe that would provide for him the stability required for achieving homeostasis.

This evolutionary drive to feel needed by others—to experience a sense of Psychological Contribution in the world—is indelibly wired into your Social Brain's neural structures. It's why we're witnessing an alarming resurgence when disenfranchised men opt to join religious, racial, and radical groups such as ISIS, the KKK, MS-13, White Nationalist groups, or—in Drake's situation—the Crips gang. In every case, it brings a return to homeostasis—the state of equanimity and balance humans strive to maintain in life. It provides these men with a sense of Psychological Contribution in the world—despite being dangerous and destructive. Pledging allegiance to these conforming tribes acts as a powerful coping system to stave off the pain and suffering experienced when boys like Drake feel— or, in some way, perceive—that society makes them unneeded and unnecessary.

The underlying dysfunction that incentivizes individuals to become radicalized is the deep desire to seek identity, purpose, and validation in a world that denies them the opportunity for expressing their contribution in life. Drake's internalized anger and anxiety that he experienced from lack of social support during his formative years became the behavioral motivation for joining the Crips. The acceptance the Crips gang provided for Drake was the proverbial drug required to satiate his need for value, belonging, and engagement. In many ways, Drake's rationale for living nearly seven years as a gang member can be viewed as another form of addiction—one driven by his despairing brain's desire for attachment to a tribe.

Returning to the concept of stress, in addition to your brain's stress-response system, there exists another vital role that stress plays when you lack homeostasis—the inflammation response. Medical science has known for quite some time your immune system is intimately linked to your body's inflammatory response, due to the invasion by biological agents—such as a bacterial infection, a cold virus, or pollen. Why's this such perilous news? Prolonged and chronic inflammation in the body is a leading factor behind a host of health issues such as the onset of certain forms of cancer, heart and lung disorders, weight gain, insomnia, skin issues, joint pain, and digestive disorders. There even exists conclusive evidence to indicate how inflammatory biomarkers are associated with mental and behavioral health issues, such as depressive disorders, and can even trigger neurodegenerative disorders like Parkinson's and Alzheimer's disease—all of which compromise your longevity and quality of life.[24]

But there's something equally fascinating about your body's inflammation process. A revolutionary study published in 2016 finds there appears to exist strong support for the correlation of social stress and your body's inflammation response. What makes this study so remarkable is that "[c]onsiderable evidence now shows that inflammatory processes and social behavior are actually powerful regulators of one another."[25] In addition to biological stress regulating the inflammation response, this study affirms there exists a co-regulation between social stress and pro-inflammatory response in the body.

Three remarkable conclusions were drawn from this ground-breaking study that are most relevant for you to know: (1) those more exposed to social stressors in life show an increase in inflammation; (2) those who experience more social isolation or report feeling lonely have increased inflammation activity; and (3) those who endure chronic social isolation are found to have a greater susceptibility to inflammation activity in response to other inflammatory triggers in the environment.[26]

In whatever way you unpack it, the study concludes the quality and extent of your social environment directly co-regulates your body's inflammation system. This pioneering research reveals the following:

[24.] Maria Almond, "Depression and inflammation: Examining the link," *Current Psychiatry*, 2013 June;12(6):24-32.

[25.] Naomi Eisenberger et al., "In Sickness and in Health: The Co-Regulation of Inflammation and Social Behavior," *Neuropsychopharmacology REVIEWS* (2016), 1–12.

[26.] Ibid.

Just as inflammatory activity can alter social behavior, so too can social behavior and features of the social environment alter inflammatory activity. Specifically, research from animal and human subjects has shown that various types of social stressors, such as those involving social separation, social defeat, social rejection, social loss, or social evaluation, can lead to transient or sometimes longer-lasting increases in proinflammatory activation.[27]

The more important question that studies such as these raise is why would your body's stress-response system create networks to alert you to social stress? Why would your body's inflammation response system become activated from social stressors? The reason again relates to the increasingly strong evidence that affirms why your brain evolved into a powerful social organ and how humans are fundamentally social beings. As the authors of this study conclude, "[G]iven the powerful role that social relationships play in our survival and the fact that social isolation makes us more vulnerable to attack and wounding, the immune system may have evolved to prepare for threats to social connection by increasing efforts towards heightened proinflammatory responses in these more vulnerable situations."[28]

On a corollary note, more studies confirm how separation trauma—especially when it occurs in children and adolescents who are suddenly or forcibly taken away from their parents or care-givers—distresses their Social Brain. What's even more remarkable is how the long-term damage produced by social neglect, abandonment, or separation can be measured and observed in the brain. It's now widely understood that the trauma experienced in children by forced separation or involuntary abandonment disrupts

---

27. Ibid.
28. Ibid.

their brain even more than the trauma endured from violence, poverty, or war.

Allow me to put the results of these research studies into more understandable and practical terms. Social stress—that results from social isolation, separation anxiety, or feeling unneeded by society—is yet another crucial factor that intimately affects your brain, body, and being. The stress you experience in each of these situations triggers your inflammation response that's linked to a host of health issues. Not only does social stress fuel the Disease of Despair by advancing anger, anxiety, and addiction, the inflammation response triggered by social stress poses one of the greatest health risks for you and society. One powerful way to achieve longevity and your Happy Brain is the regulation of your inflammation response system—which, in case you need to be reminded, happens from feeling value, belonging, and engagement to your tribe.

Getting back to Drake's story, it now reveals the neurobiological motive for his desire to join the Crips gang. Drake's Social Brain was in pain. He was likely experiencing inflammation in his body, which likely further increased his proclivity toward anger, anxiety, and addiction. Drake was operating out of his primal Stone-Age Tribe brain's drive for needing a sense of stability from being part of a welcoming tribe, which he attained from joining the Crips gang. But it backfired in his case:

> I was miserable. I was sick of living life like a barbarian. I was dying. Dying on the inside. Along with violence comes a lot of drug use and alcoholism, and I was homeless for many years. I was tired of it. But I was happy with where I was at because my street cred[ibility] was super up there. I just had to feel safe. People need that sense of belonging and that was something that I really did—it was like a drug for me. I would have given anything to have a family. In order to prove to my new family that, hey, I'm willing to

do whatever it takes to be part of this family...
and that involved violence and drugs.

On the surface, it seems inconceivable to comprehend Drake's decision to endure such a life of despair. But it makes perfect sense once viewed via the lens of evolutionary psychology and your Stone-Age Tribe brain. Drake's rationale to join the Crips gang was based on his need for stability and drive for contribution. Being part of a tribe acted like a proverbial painkiller for Drake. Knowing no other regular form of stability in his life, Drake felt compelled to remain with the Crips for all those years. Unfortunately, Drake's primal instinct for survival ultimately manifested as his Disease of Despair.

But there's good news for Drake and for you. There exists a solution to bypass the Disease of Despair. It's the Psychological Strategy of Contribution that satiates your Social Brain's thirst for feeling needed by others—by your tribe.

Contribution Creates Your Happy Brain

Your primal need to feel a sense of value, belonging, and engagement with your tribe is vital for your Social Brain and is expressed when you cultivate Psychological Contribution in your life. Whether thousands of years ago or today, your Social Brain is happiest when it knows you add *value* to your community, experience a powerful sense of *belonging* to those you love, and enjoy *engagement* from activities that benefit your tribe. But how do you make that happen? The strategy for your Happy Brain comes from living your life with purpose. *Finding your purpose in life—for your tribe—paves the path toward your Happy Brain.*

It's precisely how Drake managed to discover his sense of Psychological Contribution—and ultimately rejoice from a Happy Brain. Psychological Contribution makes you feel a necessity to and provides the powerful sense that you matter to others—your tribe. As the Dalai Lama states, "Virtually all the world's major religions teach that diligent work in the service of others is our highest nature and thus lies at the center of a happy life. Scientific surveys and studies confirm shared tenets of our faiths. Americans who prioritize doing good for others are almost twice as likely to say they are very happy about their lives."[29]

Why does this statement bear truth? It speaks to the fundamental joy you receive in knowing your contribution adds worth to your tribe and to the contentment you experience when others value your purpose in life. Whether you're a stay-at-home mom, a combat veteran, a social worker, or an emergency room doctor, your Happy Brain comes from knowing that your presence in the world matters—you add value and worth to your tribe.

The universal concept of tribe is actually embedded in the very word *contribution* that derives from the Latin verb *contribuere* "to add or bring together." In turn, Latin *contribuere* breaks down into the parts *con-* "with" and the root word *tribus* "tribe." Contribution literally means "with the tribe." Psychological Contribution is all about performing actions that add or bring value to your tribe. The word *contribution* harkens back to humanity's archaic essentiality for tribe. *Engaging in Psychological Contribution allows you to be of service to your tribe, which generates your Happy Brain.*

Even from the perspective of religion and spirituality, Psychological Contribution can be observed. The universal concept of finding your purpose and being in service to others is reflected in some form throughout all the world's religions. The spirituality behind Psychological Contribution exists in the Christian teachings of the New Testament that instruct to "press toward the mark for the prize of the high calling." It's also evident in the ancient Hindu and Buddhist concept of *dharma*—joyously fulfilling your duty in life.

Sadly, when you go through life exclusively focused on actions or indulge in behaviors that focus on maximizing your own pleasure and desires—assuming your basic survival requirements are already met in your life—it can create a profound sense of dissatisfaction in life. Your Stone-Age Tribe brain's drive for seeking transient pleasure

---

[29.] The Dalai Lama, "Dalai Lama: Behind Our Anxiety, the Fear of Being Unneeded."

that brings dissatisfaction in the present moment relates to the second Happiness Hijack: *Happiness is the anticipation of future pleasure.*

Contribution is the opposite of depression; contribution is the antidote to apathy. When the benefits that your Social Brain receives from being a valued member of a nurturing and supportive community are diminished, there exists a real danger for more of you to experience the anguish from feeling unneeded by others. When your purpose and sense of value that you bring to the world is presently absent, it's easier for you to become increasingly dissatisfied with what you do in life. You can unwittingly place your false hopes in happiness actualizing in your future, but not in the present moment.

Even worse, the suffering endured from the feeling of being unnecessary or worse—invisible—in the world is a pain too excruciating for your Social Brain. Unchecked, this anguish can lead to the unfortunate consequence of advancing more anger, anxiety, and addiction in your life and in society. Learning to embody Psychological Contribution offsets the Happiness Hijack of seeking pleasure in the future. How does it do this? It does so by fortifying you with the psychological assurance that your presence and purpose in life actively benefit others and contribute to the greater world in every given moment.

Drake's story ends on a positive and heart-lifting note. Like the Buddha thousands of years ago, who realized the source of suffering originates in your mind, Drake eventually became a "Buddha" himself. He finally awakened into the reality of how his own life of suffering was self-generated. Drake came to reclaim his Happy Brain by revaluating the circumstances of and taking responsibility for his own life.

As Drake shared with me, "My personal belief is that people can die, people can go to prison, or people can change. Those are the only three options I found at that time in my life I can actually use on a day-to-day basis." Drake came to realize why going through life as a gang member, while initially affording him immediate solace and desperate security, ultimately compromised his Happy Brain. Drake went from a despairing brain—one in which he felt resigned to a life of violence and rage in the Crips gang—to a life driven by meaning in the recovery and addiction community.

Drake's true story is one of hope; it's also a testament to the power of personal transformation you all have in the ability to claim. After nearly seven years of being homeless, dealing with drug addiction and alcoholism, and living as he calls it "the life of a barbarian," Drake is now a counselor working in a rehab center near Denver. Drake found a new and healthy tribe—one that makes him feel needed. A tribe that offers him the value, belonging, and engagement his Social Brain had been loudly crying out to receive all throughout his adolescence. Drake ultimately attained something in his life he yearned for years—balance, or what science terms *homeostasis*. What Drake lacked and what prompted him to join the Crips was to seek a state of balance, one expression of your Happy Brain.

Drake tells me he enjoys the balance in life from being in a loving relationship, serving others in need, appreciating the preciousness of life, and celebrating his fifth year of sobriety at the time of our interview. His new tribe is currently one based upon love and service, not hate and violence. When I asked Drake, "What brings you happiness at this time in your life?" this was his response, "I get this sense of happiness when I'm helping others and giving back. I get to enjoy peace because of m[y] being in the recovery community." What sustains Drake's Happy Brain is in knowing how Psychological Contribution defines his new life.

Psychological Contribution is related to finding your *dharma* and following your calling in life. It's about working not just for a weekly paycheck but working for a life's cause. What made my conversation with Drake so moving and empowering was how despite the enormity of his struggle, he has chosen to commit his life to no longer recruiting other young men into a life of misery but exposing them to a life of meaning. Drake found his higher calling and his *dharma*. Most importantly, Drake is proud to say he currently benefits from a Happy Brain. I ended my interview with Drake by asking him what does happiness mean to him at this point in life? What drives his Happy Brain? In Drake's own words, he tells me this:

> It's definitely not with money. I used to think it
> was money, and now I have enough money to

go around for a little bit. I guess where I find the truest happiness that I can ever think of is when you're sitting there and you don't have to think about a lot of stuff. It's just being grateful for being in the moment, because there were a lot of moments where I never knew if I was gonna' make it out. It's about that light at the end of the tunnel. It's about giving back as well, because I never would have what I have without those that helped me. I get to turn around and help a whole new generation of dudes I never would've associated myself with before. That's my happiness.

Like Drake, I also discovered how Psychological Contribution was evident in the immediate few days following Mom's suicide. Upon landing in Chicago and knowing Dad was unable to leave Mom's bedside where she was in a coma, two of Mom's closest friends picked me up from the airport and drove me directly to the hospital where Mom was taken the night before. They did the same for my younger brother, who arrived later that day from Philadelphia, where he was attending college at the time. For the next three days, the attentive hospital staff of nurses and doctors, our caring neighbors, along with a group of a dozen close relatives in the Chicago area were constantly and consistently there for Dad, my brother, and me.

Everything the three of us required at the time—transportation to and from the hospital, cooked meals, requisite phone calls that had to be made, along with copious amounts of solace, were given freely and abundantly without any hesitation. Everyone had his or her own specific role to play at that time. Each person was operating from a place of contribution. I felt a tremendous sense of belonging knowing how everyone was singularly dedicated to our welfare. No money was ever transacted nor asked for by anyone. My father, brother, and I knew we had others there taking charge of the situation and doing their best to help us to cope with the unfolding tragedy. This communal feeling of support I felt in knowing I had the benevolent contribution of loved ones around me at this crucial time allowed me to be present to my own suffering. This is the authentic and amazing power behind the Happiness Strategy of Contribution.

In the words of Dr. Martin Luther King Jr.: "Life's most persistent and urgent question is: What are you doing for others?" Answering that question creates your Happy Brain. Psychological Contribution makes you feel necessary to your tribe. *Experiencing Psychological Contribution benefits your tribe and nourishes your Happy Brain.*

Happy Brain Homework

Every semester of the university Happiness course noted guest speakers from diverse backgrounds are invited to the class to share their own stories of inspiration to students on what constitutes a life of happiness. In April 2017 Gopi Kallayil—Chief Evangelist, Digital Marketing at Google and author of this book's foreword—offered his words of wisdom on how finding meaning and purpose in life can become the path for achieving your Happy Brain. In an excerpt from Gopi's first book *The Internet to the Inner-Net*, he reveals the following thoughts:

> Perhaps you're thinking this sounds rather lofty. But your core purpose doesn't have to involve world peace. You may find meaning and purpose in moving mortgages or assets or dedicating yourself to your new baby, which holds more meaning for you than anything in the world. What do I mean by 'meaning' and 'purpose'? We're each blessed with unique talents and gifts. These talents might be music or sculpting or engineering. Maybe you have a gift for coaxing vegetables and flowers from seeds or organizing and orchestrating flavors and textures to create an amazing meal for your family. You might

have the ability to make people feel good about themselves, or you're a natural caregiver, or you're great with kids and teach kindergarten. It doesn't matter. Everyone is uniquely blessed.[30]

What Gopi expresses in his language conveys the essence behind the Psychological Strategy of Contribution. The key to your Happy Brain isn't so much about *figuring out the purpose of life, but rather expressing your purpose in life.*

Here's another Happy Brain homework for you that I call "Sharing Your Gifts" exercise. I invite you to wake up tomorrow morning and every morning and ask yourself the question: "What's one simple action I can take today that brings value to others?" Perhaps this is a question you can encourage your partner, spouse, friends, or children to answer: "How do I get to express my talents and gifts to the world today? What can I do to make one other person feel valuable and needed today?" To help you in this daily exercise, you're welcome to chronicle your specific acts in your personal "Happy Brain" journal by visiting www.ScienceofaHappyBrain.com.

Whoever you are or no matter what you were taught to believe, every one of you has a purpose in life to fulfill. Actualizing that purpose in your life derives from Psychological Contribution. It doesn't always have to be measured by *how much money* it brings to you. Psychological Contribution is measured by *how much meaning* it brings to you. While a flight attendant, construction worker, an elementary school teacher, hotel maid, and emergency room doctor have various levels of income, each provides a valuable service to the world. In this sense, you rightfully experience Psychological Contribution in your own unique way.

Psychological Contribution is all about knowing how your presence in the world matters and how others would feel your absence. Expressing Psychological Contribution also doesn't require you to become the next Nelson Mandela or Malala Yousafzai. Acts

---

[30.] Gopi Kallayil, *The Internet to the Inner-Net: Five Ways to Reset Your Connection and Live a Conscious Life* (Hay House, Inc., 2015), 65-66.

of contribution and of service can be as simple as holding the door for a disabled or elderly person or volunteering to serve food once a month at your local food shelter. Of course, since you fundamentally evolved to become a social being, Psychological Contribution is best enjoyed with others. Your Social Brain thrives the most when you contribute and collaborate toward a common goal—whether cooking a meal together as a family, clearing up the neighborhood park with your fraternity, or building shelters for the homeless as a community. These are all powerful acts that help you manifest Psychological Contribution. Acts of service and of contribution further enrich the Happy Brain for you and others—the form of happiness where everyone wins. Every action, no matter how insignificant, is an expression of the Happiness Strategy of Contribution.

Bonus Content

- Visit www.ScienceofaHappyBrain.com and begin to apply the Happiness Strategy of Contribution into your own life in order to enjoy the benefits of a Happy Brain.
- Write down and keep track of how your own "Sharing Your Gifts" exercise boosts your Happy Brain.

LESSON EIGHT

THE HAPPINESS STRATEGY OF CONNECTION

When we suffer in silence, we think that we are alone, different, separate. When we share our stories of suffering, we find that we are the same.
—Vironoka Teguleva

Our Age of Disconnection

One afternoon in the small Missouri town of Park Mills, Marleen arrived back home, unaware of how a simple letter was about to change her life and become the impetus for her to experience a Happy Brain. Marleen was surprised to discover a mysterious handwritten envelope among her mail. She recognized the return address on the envelope was actually from a home on the same street—a few doors down and just across the road—but she had no idea who the occupant of that home was. Marleen's curiosity was piqued. Inside the envelope was a personally penned note that read: "Would you consider to become my friend? I'm 90 years old—live alone and all my friends have passed away. I'm so lonesome and scared. Please—I pray for someone"[31] While the letter contained just a few lines, it spoke volumes to Marleen's soul.

Marleen's eyes began to water reading this tender note, as it triggered memories of her own dear grandmother, who sadly died all alone in hospice. The heartache Marleen felt reflecting on her own grandmother's suffering and passing away in solitude is what prompted Marleen the next day to grab another friend and some cupcakes and head over to meet the mystery person who wrote the anguished letter.

Wanda heard the knock on the door and opened to see who was there. When she did, the ninety-year-old woman's heart jumped with a mixture of relief, joy, and surprise. Wanda didn't expect her neighbor to respond; in fact, Wanda didn't think anyone would respond to her letter. Inviting Marleen and her friend inside, Wanda confessed, "I hope you didn't think I was stupid for writing you, but I had to do something. Thank you so much for coming over. I've lived here for fifty years and don't know any of my neighbors." If you need any further evidence why we're a society suffering from the Disease of Despair, it's Wanda. Her story reflects the importance behind why you require the Social Strategy of Connection to experience your Happy Brain in life.

There is a grave and growing health crisis facing society today that contributes to the Disease of Despair. This danger is humanity's Age of Disconnection. While society gives tremendous attention to biological and psychological health issues—such as smoking, addiction, anxiety, diabetes, depression, dementia, and cancer to name a few—there's a silent killer out there that's damaging the welfare and well-being of millions of people around the world. That killer is social isolation.

While on the surface, social isolation might not seem like such a serious health crisis, but social isolation is a grave issue affecting millions of people around the world who report feeling greater levels of loneliness and disconnection. Social isolation does more than

---

[31.] Tara Bahrampour, "This is what happened when a lonely 90-year-old wrote a letter to a stranger," *The Washington Post*, Aug. 30, 2017.

compromise your biological and psychological health; it equally impacts your spiritual health. When left unchecked, social isolation can produce spiritual desolation—another factor that adversely affects your well-being and outlook onto the world when your life lacks meaning and hope.

The happiness Wanda received on that day of Marleen's visit was a form of therapy no pill nor medication could replicate. It's precisely Wanda's true story of yearning for social contact that exemplifies the wound of a world agonizing in an Age of Disconnection and the millions suffering from a despairing brain. While many groups suffer from the damage caused by social deprivation, there exists one particular segment of society that's exceptionally vulnerable to the health hazards posed from living in an Age of Disconnection—the rising number of the "orphaned elderly" like Wanda.

While it's often the tendency to associate orphans as children, there's a disturbingly growing segment of the elderly population in the United States, who are aging alone and going through life socially scared and psychologically scarred. These elderly orphans are often childless, widowed, or have no immediate relatives in their area. At present, it's estimated nearly one-quarter of Americans over the age of sixty-five currently fall into this category. Making matters worse, the number of aging Baby Boomers is expected to keep this statistic dangerously on the rise.[32] This is truly a looming health crisis in the making.

To help you fully grasp the gravity behind this issue, noted primate biologist Frans De Waal declares, "Our bodies and minds are made for social life, and we become hopelessly depressed in its absence. This is why next to death, solitary confinement is our worst punishment."[33] It's perfect sense why countries that abolished the death penalty employ solitary confinement as the next most severe form of punishment. When nurturing social contacts are lacking in

---

[32]. James Hood, "Free-living Baby Boomers at risk of becoming 'elderly orphans,'" *Consumer Affairs*, May 18, 2015.

[33]. Frans De Waal, *The Age of Empathy: Nature's Lessons for a Kinder Society* (Broadway Books, 1st edition, 2010).

your life, the result is a fate as painful as death. In the absence of tribe, you suffer in solitude.

It's the reason why Wanda's story is felt so strongly. The saddest aspect of her situation is how society tacitly condemns Wanda and the millions of elderly Americans like her to the cruelty of a life forced into solitary confinement. Regardless of medical caregivers coming to Wanda's home daily to monitor her health and check up on the oxygen tank she uses to breathe, Wanda has rarely left her home in seven years. Wanda painfully realized a profound truth: Despite the best intentions of her paid medical help, caregivers aren't the same as having people that simply just care about you.

In today's world of chaos and conflict, of anger and anxiety, you need the social stability and collective security that tribe brings now more than ever. In just the past few decades, society has been slowly going against what required nature thousands of years for you to become—a social being endowed with a Social Brain that evolved for connectivity and community as a strategy for survival.

The start of the twenty-first century marked the dawn of the new millennium and birthed today's Age of Digitalization. While many of you enjoy the indispensable benefits and advantages from living in a digital world and an interconnected planet, the rapidly accelerating world of digital dependence comes at a heavy price society is paying for dearly—the Age of Disconnection. Digital technology connects you virtually online, but it sadly disconnects you personally in real time. The Age of Digitalization ushers in society's Age of Disconnection, whereby you gradually are losing the primal experience of real-time and physical connection with others.

Tribe has gradually become the equivalent of an "endangered species" over the past few decades. Today's Age of Disconnection leaves you grappling for a profound sense of meaning in life, creates a generation desperately yearning for purpose, and accelerates a technological society craving inner truth in a tsunami of digital information.

The Age of Disconnection currently manifests as two grave social perils—it promotes a lifestyle of *psychological individualism* and produces a culture of *social isolationism*. You can think of psychological individualism exemplified by the motto of "go it alone and do it yourself" that underscores the notion you have to rely only on yourself in order to make it in the world. Unfortunately, it's this established narrative of psychological individualism that society idolizes as the standard benchmark for strength and success. Psychological individualism is one factor from humanity's Age of Disconnection that triggers the Disease of Despair and sabotages your Happy Brain.

The other is social isolationism—the twin to psychological individualism—reflected in the "suck it up and tough it out" attitude that can pressure you into bottling up your pain, encouraging you to shut down emotionally, and isolating physically when burdened with hardship or hurt. Think of psychological individualism and social isolationism as two cognitive biases society convinces you to accept as truths.

But the reality, the cultural narrative behind both psychological individualism and social isolationism projects the façade of believing you're mandated to go through the travails of life on your own without the support and assistance from others—from your tribe. Contrary to what society might have you believe, evolution never primed humans for psychological individualism and social isolationism, for neither is a strategy for the continued survival of the human species. If they were, humanity would've perished thousands of years ago. Junger provides more thoughts on why psychological individualism and social isolationism exist today—along with their consequences:

> First agriculture, and then industry, changed two fundamental things about the human experience. The accumulation of personal property allowed people to make more and more individualistic choices about their lives, and those choices unavoidably diminished group efforts toward a common good. And as society modernized, people found themselves able to live independently from

any communal group…They can be surrounded
by others and yet feel deeply, dangerously alone.[34]

Yet, there's another malicious message implied by psychological individualism and social isolationism—asking for help or reaching out to others in times of crisis is somehow construed as a sign of emotional weakness or a moral failure. In the numerous trainings I conduct for mental health-care professionals, I know all too well how a social stigma exists—perpetuated by a culturally accepted belief system—when society labels you a "loser" when asking for support or seeking help from others.

It's the perceived fear of being stereotyped as frail or flawed in some way by society that becomes a major obstacle why those who suffer from mental illness, behavioral disorders, PTSD, or even social solitude can often feel reluctant to seek out vital support and necessary assistance. The shame and judgment that society often projects when you desperately require the safety and support from others—your tribe—further fuel psychological individualism and social isolationism in society. How does this all pertain to your Happy Brain?

Humanity's Age of Disconnection has produced a generation that dangerously normalizes psychological individualism and social isolationism. They've become culturally accepted social behaviors that have morphed into deceptively positive attributes for society. In actuality, both psychological individualism and social isolationism have the opposite effect—they compound the Disease of Despair and stunt your Happy Brain.

Most alarming of all, the Age of Disconnection is one in which you may even experience a profound disconnection from your authentic sense of self-worth and detach from the value you bring to the world—to your tribe. I lecture and travel quite extensively and witness firsthand how society's Age of Disconnection leaves many of you struggling, scared, and sad. Today's Age of Disconnection finds you living in an age of anger, anxiety, and addiction.

[34.] Junger, *Tribe*, 18.

It's the very reason why living in an Age of Disconnection raises the alarm for many pundits who document the shocking increase in today's Disease of Despair—ominously reflected by the spike in rates of suicide, depression, PTSD, anxiety, lower life spans, and addiction over the past decade. What's even more disturbing, the Disease of Despair is especially rampant in economically developed and technologically advanced nations that epitomize the economic pinnacle of wealth and abundance. What that means, money and prosperity don't immunize you from the Disease of Despair. Why? Money and material goods are no substitute for your greatest wealth in life—belonging to a tribe.

Thomas Friedman reveals precisely this sentiment in his recent book *Thank You for Being Late*, in which he interviews former US Surgeon General Dr. Vivek Murthy. Friedman recounts in his book a poignant conversation he once had with Murthy:

> [W]hat was the biggest disease in America today, without hesitation [Murthy] answered: 'It's not cancer. It's not heart disease. It's *isolation*. It is the pronounced isolation that so many people are experiencing that is the great pathology of our lives today.' How ironic. We are the most technologically connected generation in human history—and yet more people feel isolated more than ever. This only reinforces Murthy's earlier point—that the connections that matter most, and are in most short supply today, are the human-to-human ones.[35]

While you likely know of the tremendous health risks posed to your longevity from improper diet, lack of exercise, insufficient sleep, chronic stress, and other behaviors such as smoking and excessive drinking, science is now exposing a shocking truth about the human condi-

---

[35] Thomas Friedman, *Thank You for Being Late: An Optimist's Guide to Thriving in the Age of Accelerations* (Farrar, Straus and Giroux, 2016), 450-1.

tion. Social isolation appears to be another alarming health catastrophe plaguing humanity. Despite the rapid technological increases in digital connectivity, the current Age of Disconnection deters the "human-to-human" connections we evolved for as a species—the longing within each of you to be part of a strong, nurturing tribe.

Take More Vitamin S

Getting back to Wanda's story, her medical attendants, who regularly checked in on her, were expertly supplying oxygen and medication to address Wanda's physical and biological needs. But the medicine Wanda found herself woefully deficient in is your Social Brain's life-enhancing nutrient—Vitamin S (Vitamin Social). Vitamin S is nature's antidote to psychological individualism and social isolationism. Vitamin S is the nutrient most lacking in today's Age of Disconnection. The lack of Vitamin S in Wanda's Social Brain compelled her to write her plea to Marleen. It's the lack of Vitamin S in your life that malnourishes your Social Brain; regular doses of Vitamin S nourish your Happy Brain.

Here's the crucial question you need to be asking. Knowing how the health risks posed by psychological individualism and social isolationism are tangibly real, why is it no one knew the depth of Wanda's despair? It's basically because many people tend to ignore—or haven't been educated enough to be aware of—the signs and symptoms of depression caused by social deprivation when you lack tribe.

Luckily, the significance of social connection and the value it bears on achieving balance, longevity, and resilience is increasingly being investigated by the medical community. My colleague and friend, Dr. Michael Irwin, at UCLA's Semel Institute for Neuroscience and Human Behavior, details evidence of the medical consequences that social isolation imposes on the elderly. In a 2015 published review, he and his fellow researchers advance this finding:

> Older adults often experience social isolation which may have a profound negative effect on

their behavioral health... The findings of this systematic review suggest that social isolation in late life may indeed increase behavioral symptoms such as sleep disturbance, depression, and fatigue. Moreover, the effects of subjective social isolation, compared to objective social isolation, may contribute more significantly to sleep disturbance and depressive symptoms.[36]

This study exposes why Wanda's brain was operating as a despairing brain. Due to the social isolation she was experiencing, her Social Brain was mimicking the pain felt from the social distress produced by years of social deprivation, as if it were actual physical pain. Wanda's fate perfectly captures the Happiness Equation learned earlier. If you want to know the fundamental reason why Wanda, as a last resort, wrote a note of desperation to Marleen, it can be viewed in this variation of the Happiness Equation:

Attachment to Tribe = Social Brain = Happy Brain
Abandonment from Tribe = Solitary Brain = Despairing Brain

The anguish Wanda wrote in her letter opens a window into the *Bio-Psycho-Socio-Spiritual* nature of stress and its relationship to your Social Brain. Prolonged social isolation and emotional loneliness produce your Solitary Brain—the antithesis of your Social Brain that took evolution thousands of years to create. Wanda's Solitary Brain left her no other choice but to act.

On a personal note, if you have elderly neighbors or know senior citizens who live alone, please visit or regularly check in on them. I assure that both you and they will greatly benefit from a strong and healthy dose of Vitamin S.

---

36. H. Choi, M.R. Irwin, and H.J. Cho, "Impact of social isolation on behavioral health in elderly: Systematic review," *World Journal of Psychiatry*, 2015;5(4):432-8. Published 2015 Dec 22. doi:10.5498/wjp.v5.i4.432.

What Wanda's Solitary Brain was craving more than anything else was Vitamin S, in the form of social contact with her tribe. It explains why Wanda, in an aggravated state of stress, wrote her note of despair to Marleen. It's a sad fate knowing how there are millions of people, just like Wanda, who are anguishing from the pain of a Solitary Brain. We're a nation woefully deficient in Vitamin S, and society now pays a heavy price.

One proven strategy neurobiology affirms for you to achieve long-lasting happiness is to nourish your brain with the important Vitamin S. Tribe and social bonding is the Vitamin S you require for survival—the primal nutrient that nourishes and strengthens your Happy Brain. Let's reveal the mechanism evolution wired into your brain why Vitamin S is crucial for helping you achieve balance, longevity, and resilience.

Connection Creates Your Happy Brain

What do baptisms and bar mitzvahs, barbecues and Burning Man have in common? They represent the diverse ways you express tribe. While all these activities create community and your Happy Brain, there's another reason why socialization is witnessed throughout every culture and is a core feature of human behavior. Knowing you belong to a tribe is how your Social Brain rewards you with happiness in the form of Vitamin S. As renowned Harvard social biologist Wilson affirms, "People must have a tribe. It gives them a name in addition to their own social meaning in a chaotic world. It makes the environment less disorienting and dangerous."[37] Tribe is the Social Strategy of Connection required for you to enjoy the benefits of a Happy Brain.

If you recall the "dessert-eating" exercise from a few lessons ago, the anticipation from eating food produces a powerful release of the neurotransmitter dopamine into your body that you experience as the

---

[37.] Edward O. Wilson, *The Social Conquest of Earth* (Liverlight Publishing Corporation 2012), 57.

sensation of pleasure. While food is a biological necessity for survival, there exists another potent reason why food became such a staple of human behavior. The communion over food and the act of cooking together continue to reflect the power from Social Connection. For your Social Brain—that views the world through connection and community—eating food together reinforces the happiness from being part of a tribe. Again, your Stone-Age Tribe brain is focused on the "me," while the Social Brain is focused on the "we."

Throughout history, eating has become an important daily ritual where all members of your tribe gather to celebrate the pleasure of eating as a community. And it's more than just the nightly family dinner or Sunday brunch with friends. Your Social Brain is the very reason why throughout the world's religious traditions meals and sacred repasts endure and play a central role in the rituals and celebrations of people from all faiths—whether it's the Muslim *Iftar*, Jewish *Seder*, Christian *Easter*, or a wedding banquet. It's why national holidays such as Thanksgiving and the Fourth of July revolve around the festivity of food and community—your tribe.

Of course, you know this to be true. Where's the most popular place for you and your friends *always* to hang out at parties? The kitchen. Do you ever wonder why that is? The sights, sounds, and smells of food express Social Connection with your tribe. The ancient art of cooking and rejoicing together over meals creates attachment to tribe that your Social Brain equates to happiness. Let's explore the brain science behind why your Social Brain comes to experience the pleasure you get from food just as strongly as the pleasure you get from Social Connection.

You were introduced in an earlier lesson to the evolutionary strategy why experiencing pleasure became wired into your Stone-Age Tribe brain. From the lens of evolutionary psychology, seeking communion with your tribe reinforces your brain's pleasure reward circuits. Let's focus in more detail on your brain's dopaminergic-reward system and the neurobiology behind why experiencing pleasure became vital for human survival.

Your brain's built-in anticipatory reward mechanism for motivating you to continue actions—no matter their challenge or hardship—became the evolutionary origin of pleasure. This is again the reason why your brain craves pleasure—it became a crucial strategy for survival of the species. In the absence of your brain's dopaminergic-reward system and the dopaminergic neurons in your brain, there'd be no incentive for you to continue to eat, have sex, sleep, bear children, and—most importantly—to socialize.

In this way, the neurotransmitter dopamine governs your behavior behind motivation, anticipation, and reward. The dopaminergic-reward system solidifies behaviors such as sex and eating as vital strategies for survival that you associate as highly pleasurable experiences. It also accounts for the fact that while "dopaminergic neurons account for less than 1% of the total neuronal population of the brain, they have a profound effect on brain function."[38] If only minuscule amounts of dopaminergic neurons exist in your brain, what makes them so crucial for survival? How do they relate to your Happy Brain? It all goes back to the Social Brain model. As you're rapidly discovering, the drive to know you're loved, valued, and cared for by others is as fundamental to your balance, longevity, and resilience as are food, water, warmth, and sleep. What follows is the medical study that reveals why Social Connection promotes your Happy Brain.

In a 2013 experiment conducted by Eisenberger and Inagaki, subjects who self-reported experiencing feelings of loneliness were placed in an fMRI scanner. Unbeknownst to the test subject, an important person in his or her life—a parent, co-worker, sibling, friend, etc.—was asked to write two letters. One letter simply stated obvious facts about the test subject, while the other letter detailed specific positive personal qualities about the participant. For example, one letter describes objective observations, such as, "You have curly hair. You are a tall person." While the other letter from the same writer might say, "You made me so happy marrying my son. I'm grateful you're the godparent to my child. I love you for being my best friend all these years."

[38.] Arias-Carrión et. al., "The Dopaminergic-reward system."

Not knowing what the letters contained, the test subjects were then placed in an fMRI scanner and asked to read each letter—the factual one and the emotional one—while their brains were being scanned in real-time. It came as no surprise to the researchers how the brain responded differently when test subjects read each different style of letter. But that wasn't the intention of this study. The real goal behind the experiment was to locate the precise region and measure the intensity of activity in the brain when test subjects read the more personalized letters of emotional recognition and praise. The results surprised the researchers.

When subjects, who again previously self-reported feelings of loneliness, were reading the letters of positive emotional valence, there occurred a pronounced increase of activity in a specific region of the brain—the ventral striatum. The researchers were reasonably surprised to observe this region of the brain firing for one astonishing reason: a function of your ventral striatum is to regulate food-cravings. The study conjectured when people who report loneliness read letters that made them feel emotionally valued and socially acknowledged, their brains experienced an equally strong craving—a yearning for Social Connection.[39]

What makes this experiment relevant to your everyday life? Why does it matter for your Happy Brain? It appears your ventral striatum governs both your craving for food and friendship. Why would your brain do so? One suggestion is that it aligns precisely with the Social Brain hypothesis—the evolutionary necessity of socialization is just as crucial for your survival as is food for your health and longevity. Despite differences between tangible physical rewards (food) versus intangible emotional rewards (affection), your Social Brain evolved to react similarly when it craves sugar or seeks Social Connection. As the ventral striatum is part of your brain's dopaminergic-reward system, your brain experiences the longing for the sweetness of sugar and for the satiety of socialization in the same way.

---

[39] Tristen Inagaki and Naomi Eisenberger, "Shared Neural Mechanisms Underlying Social Warmth and Physical Warmth," *Psychological Science*. 013 24: 2272 originally published online 18 September 2013.

To better understand the relationship among Social Connection, pleasure, behavioral reward, and motivation, this is what you need to know. Eating chocolate cake and being told "I love you" activate your ventral striatum and the dopaminergic neurons that make you experience pleasure. You feel immense pleasure from both sugary candy and Social Connection. While the former might lack nutritional value, Social Connection nourishes your brain with Vitamin S.

But here's another powerful revelation about your brain. Just as there exist overlapping regions of your brain that process physical pain (a broken bone) and social pain (a broken bond), there equally exists a shared system in your brain that experiences physical pleasure (food) and social pleasure (connection). This strategy of your Social Brain explains why you crave camaraderie and thirst for tribe just as much as you desire food and drink. Whether it's love, affection, or praise, Social Connection nourishes your Happy Brain as powerfully as food does for advancing balance, longevity, and resilience.

Evolution developed an innovative strategy for overcoming the unpredictability and paucity faced by your ancient Stone-Age ancestors—Social Connection. Banding together into groups for security and safety provided early humans with two key elements for survival. The first is the predictability in knowing you are always part of a community whose foremost priority is the safety and security of all members. The second is how Social Connection diminishes your Stone-Age Tribe brain's primal fear of scarcity.

For your early Stone-Age ancestors, the fear of scarcity is not just established around the lack of food or resources, but around the fear of scarcity from Social Connection. Your anticipation for a reward over the prospect of consuming food triggers the same region of your brain over your longing for social attachment with others.

Most of you would agree how there's great pleasure in taking that first bite of your favorite dessert. Brain science research equally affirms why the pleasure experienced from indulging your sweet tooth activates shared regions of your brain when you see a special loved one. But here's a question for you: Given the option between never being able to eat dessert—or something equally as pleasurable—or never being able to enjoy social contact with your loved ones, which would you give up? Your Social Brain has very little need for chocolate or cheesecake, but it would atrophy and die from malnourishment without Social Connection.

The lack of in-person social engagement—again, social media and virtual connection don't count here—is one reason for the increase in today's Disease of Despair. Society's Age of Disconnection triggers greater anger, anxiety, and addiction that is the product of the next Happiness Hijack: *Happiness is an individual pursuit, not a collective one.*

This pervasive sabotage to your happiness is reflected in society that normalizes psychological individualism and social isolationism. When the ability to belong to a nourishing and supportive tribe is absent from your life, the resulting lack of Social Connection poses a grave threat to your well-being. Additionally, this Happiness Hijack deceives you into believing happiness is an individual pursuit and one disassociated from societal happiness that ultimately sabotages your Happy Brain.

It's now indisputable—humans evolved for Social Connection. Nature reinforces the importance of social bonding through the brain's release of dopamine to reward you whenever you participate in any form of pro-social behavior. You feel good when you connect; your Social Brain gifts you with a massive boost of dopamine every time you choose to meet face to face with friends over coffee, celebrate the holidays with family, and create space in your life for playtime. The dopaminergic-reward system is another evolutionary ploy of your Social Brain that relates to the Social Strategy of Connection that produces the crucial Vitamin S required for your Happy Brain.

This is how Social Connection played out for me during that time in my life when I learned the news of Mom's suicide. That period in my life as a first-year doctoral student was hectic and busy. As a young adult living on my own thousands of miles away from my parents and with my brother on the opposite end of the country in college, I was admittedly negligent in keeping regular social contact with my family as in the past. Even up to that point in my life, it's safe to say my relationship with Dad was never as strong and robust as it was with Mom. Even my brother and I, who were normally very close, didn't communicate as often as I would've liked. I suppose I could blame it on the consequences from living in an age before email, social media, and texts; but the reality is the demands of graduate school and enjoying my sense of independence certainly factored into my lack of communication.

But hearing the news of Mom and knowing how the three of us—my father, brother, and me—immediately had to rally in order to be there for Mom, all emotional barriers among us quickly evaporated. The walls that were built over the years between Dad and me broke down on that day seeing Mom in a coma at the hospital. What mattered most to the three of us was the common bond we equally had for Mom. Being able to commune in our shared love for Mom and be there for each other in our collective time of need precisely embodies the Social Strategy of Connection. *Experiencing Social Connection is the Vitamin S that sustains your Happy Brain.*

Happy Brain Homework

Here's another exercise you hopefully will benefit from that underscores the power of Social Connection in your life. It's the "Remembering Happy Times" exercise. I want you to recall your twenty-first birthday—or any significant birthday or event like your high-school graduation party or wedding day. I now challenge you to remember as many gifts you received on that day. Take a couple of minutes and see how you do.

Any luck? How many gifts did you bring to mind? Most of you can perhaps remember some of the presents that stand out—like a new china set as a wedding present or a new phone for a special birthday—however, most of you probably find it really hard to recollect every specific physical present you received that day.

Are you ready to try something else? I now want you to recall as many people as possible in attendance at this same event that you brought to mind. Specifically, what memorable words did people say to you, what were they wearing, was there a special cake or meal everyone enjoyed, or can you picture the exact place where your event took place? I strongly suspect you're more easily able to answer those questions. Why is it that you more readily remember experiences, places, and people in your life, while it's much harder to list the objects and material goods that you've acquired or received throughout your life? Because pleasure isn't the same as happiness.

It's precisely because of this truism why this exercise works. It also exposes another fundamental aspect about your Social Brain and human behavior—experiences that generate the sensation of pleasure are fleeting. So why is this a problem? There's a tendency in society to conflate pleasure as happiness. Here's how I discuss it in my first book *Brain, Body & Being*:

> While most of us strive to feel happy, many of us remain stuck on the path of pleasure. I concede that happiness is a vague term, personally defined, culturally relative and, in many ways, a social construct. But just because people confuse happiness with pleasure, the brain does not... Things that tend to bring us pleasure are all fleeting experiences. Once the feeling of pleasure is gone, we yearn for the next time we'll have it. Happiness, however, is a state that is independent of an external situation or experience. Happiness can even be triggered by a mere thought or memory.[40]

Here's another way to look at it: *Pleasure has a limited shelf life; happiness has no expiration date.* You don't have to be someone who specializes in brain science and behavioral health to understand this powerful concept. Pleasure is a temporary sensation; happiness is an enduring state. Chocolate cake, birthday presents, a cold beer, and a massage are all pleasurable experiences that are linked to your brain's dopaminergic-reward system. So, too, are addictive behaviors

---

[40]. Kumar, *Brain, Body & Being*, 11.

such as compulsive shopping, gambling, excessive drinking, smoking, overeating, or abusing drugs. The sensation of pleasure you get from each of these activities, however, fades quickly...until the next time it occurs. Compare these actions to experiences such as taking your kids on a camping trip, hiking with your best friend, playing with your dog at the beach, or celebrating a family reunion. While it's true these are also temporary activities, there's one important distinction—the memories of joy you associate with these experiences will never fade. It's why I repeat—*pleasure has a temporary shelf life; happiness has no expiration date.* If you want to enjoy the benefits of a Happy Brain, focus on experiences that are grounded in Social Connection. It's precisely what you and your brain love most and do best—connect.

Bonus Content

- Visit www.ScienceofaHappyBrain.com and apply the Happiness Strategy of Connection into your own life in order to enjoy the benefits of your Happy Brain.
- Read the entirety of Wanda's touching letter and watch her full story.
- Learn tools to manage your Happy Brain in our Age of Disconnection.

LESSON NINE

THE HAPPINESS STRATEGY OF COMPASSION

If we want to create a viable, peaceful world,
we've got to integrate compassion into the gritty
realities of 21st century life.

—Karen Armstrong

In a Crisis, We Tribe

Vincent Ardolino doesn't strike you as a man you'd readily describe as warm and fuzzy or as a hardened New Yorker easily overcome with emotion. Ardolino, though, is a man who speaks from his heart and whose words choke when recounting one of the most memorable days of his life—September 11, 2001. On a day most Americans associate with despair and tragedy, for Ardolino, it was also the day he unexpectedly found the meaning behind a Happy Brain. How did this happen? On this fateful day, Ardolino was reminded of humanity's timeless power and enduring resilience that manifest the moment we become a tribe. Here's Ardolino in his own words:

> Housewives, workers who do windows, we had executives. And the thing that was the best, everyone helped everyone… I was compelled [to act], as I'm the type of person who can't stand by

and watch other people suffer. And to me they were suffering. They wanted to get off the island. And there was no way for them to get off the island, other than the water.[41]

Ardolino is recounting his participation in Operation Boatlift. For those unfamiliar with this event, it's the heroic tale that transpired in the aftermath of the 9/11 terrorist attacks on the World Trade Towers. Many of you might be familiar with the historic World War II Dunkirk evacuation—popularized by the 2017 film *Dunkirk*—that witnessed the heroic naval rescue of stranded British soldiers from the French seaside town of Dunkerque in 1940 by a fleet of English volunteer vessels. While the epic and arduous events of this famous battle will be forever memorialized by humanity, Operation Boatlift has the distinct recognition of being the largest known water evacuation believed to have happened in history. While roughly 350,000 soldiers were rescued at the Battle of Dunkirk over the course of *nine days*, Operation Boatlift saved the souls of nearly 500,000 New Yorkers in the course of just *nine hours*.

Trapped from the disaster site and chaos from the assault, every official and public mode of transportation—bridges, tunnels, subways, trains, and mass transit—to allow entry into and exit out from the island of Manhattan closed down due to heightened security alerts and the fear of other possible acts of terrorism. For the nearly one million people who commute daily for work to the Island of Manhattan, they were left trapped and with no immediate means of escape.

As a result, at the site of the attack on the southern tip of Manhattan, hundreds of thousands of souls recently traumatized from the tumult and chaos were left stranded and scared. Compounding to the sheer panic and confusion people felt, a dense cloud of toxic smoke and ash ominously began to envelope the Wall Street district in all directions. Utterly helpless amidst the impenetrable debris cloud

---

[41]. Eddie Rosenstein, "BOATLIFT, An Untold Tale of 9/11 Resilience," *RoadtoResilience*

and not knowing how even to get home, frantic Manhattan residents and daily commuters were confronted by an extra challenge—the possibility of having to walk arduous hours to seek the refuge and safety of being with their loved ones.

What makes Operation Boatlift so powerful is without even any hesitation or consideration for their safety, Ardolino and over a hundred civilian captains instinctively knew what had to be done. Ardolino and his fellow "Boatlifters" from the greater New York metropolitan area organized an impromptu fleet of volunteer ships with one goal in mind—to evacuate the hordes of stranded survivors from the carnage that was unfolding on Wall Street. Why did they act? To rescue their tribe. The instinctive ability that allows you to identify and empathize over the welfare of others—from loved ones to complete strangers—is the Spiritual Strategy of Compassion.

It was apparent very quickly how boats—a mode of transportation overlooked or readily dismissed by many modern-day New Yorkers—suddenly became the only available means to evacuate Lower Manhattan. At first it was just a handful of volunteer vessels that happened to be in the vicinity of Wall Street to begin rescuing the marooned and frantic civilians. The US Coast Guard fathomed very quickly this was a crisis beyond anything they'd ever anticipated or trained for in drills. The magnitude and gravity of the situation required a drastic response. An official distress call went out by the Coast Guard urgently requesting for any and all available vessels in the New York metropolitan area to converge at the southern seaboard of Wall Street where thousands of people were flocking to escape the carnage.

The Coast Guard had no idea who would respond, but the call was heard—in force and in numbers no one expected. In the matter of mere minutes, hundreds of patrol ships, corporate crafts, fishing boats, diving ships, private vessels, and small tugs formed an impromptu flotilla to remove quickly and safely the stranded survivors from Ground Zero, who were scrambling to get away from the hellish scene unfolding. More amazing, the successful evacuation was executed organically and without the need for any formal or strategic planning. How could this be possible for an event of this scope and scale?

As Boatlifter Jones proudly explains, "You couldn't have planned nothin' to happen that fast, that quick... No training, this was just people doing what they had to do. Average people—they stepped up when they needed to." Flashing a smile of pride, Jones recounts, "They showed me that when American people need to come together and pull together, they will do it."[42]

Everyone has surely heard the many profound stories of hope, courage, and sacrifice behind the incredible and tragic events transpiring on 9/11, but there's something far more extraordinary about Operation Boatlift than meets the eye. While 9/11 will forever be etched in our collective psyche as a day of panic and horror, something else remarkable and inspiring occurred on that fateful day. Operation Boatlift reveals a core quality of our human identity, of you, and of everyone you know—when pushed to the limit and with little choice, your brain evolved for pro-social actions and altruistic behaviors that ensure the safety and security of your tribe. It's again another proof to the power of the Social Brain that played out on 9/11 with Operation Boatlift.

Stephen Flynn, former US Coast Guard officer and executive producer of the short documentary film *Boatlift*, encapsulates this concept by saying, "We wanted to tell a story that reminds Americans that this is a country that bounces back from adversity... Our national DNA is resilience. The key for us is to move forward with some key lessons and one of the lessons missing is the strength of civil society and how it responded when 9/11 happened."[43] Flynn, Ardolino, and Jones reveal the same, timeless truth—the power of Spiritual Compassion and the potency behind tribe.

So why am I sharing the true story of Operation Boatlift with you? Operation Boatlift is a modern-day testament to the unrecognized source of your Happy Brain—your tribe. Unfortunately,

---

42. Katharine Herrup, "Boatlifters: The unknown story of 9/11," *Reuters*, Sept. 11, 2011.
43. Ibid.

the importance and value of tribe are mostly ignored in a world that praises psychological individualism, prioritizes social isolationism, promotes our Age of Disconnection, and produces your Solitary Brain.

Yet Operation Boatlift is a timeless social snapshot that illuminates wisdom advanced throughout the ages and reveals a long-forgotten secret for you to claim a Happy Brain. In times of tragedy and in moments of strife there exists an evolutionary drive for you to rush to the aid of others—your tribe. Operation Boatlift reminds you of a valuable piece about our shared human identity and collective past that's woefully absent in contemporary society's Age of Disconnection. *Tribe is a Bio-Psycho-Socio-Spiritual strategy required for your Happy Brain.* Why do I believe so?

Sometimes it takes a crisis to remember what's *biologically* wired into your brain, *psychologically* imprinted into your consciousness, *socially* encoded in your DNA, and *spiritually* embodied in your heart—tribe. Operation Boatlift is an event that succeeded for one reason alone. Every Boatlifter on 9/11 was instinctually operating as a tribe—the quintessential feature of what makes you human and the foundation for your Happy Brain.

Boatlifter Kirk Slater sums it up perfectly: "It's just human nature. You see people in distress on the sea wall in Manhattan begging you to pick them up. You have to...you have to pick them up."[44] His words and the actions of everyone who played a role in Operation Boatlift exemplify the potency of tribe that reflects a timeless testament about human nature—in times of crisis, we do the right thing. It's what the tribe demands. *In a crisis, we tribe.*

Bodega owners and five-star chefs, corporate executives and construction workers, schoolteachers and single moms helped each other onto boats without question. On 9/11, status, income, titles, and degrees made no difference. No one had inherently more worth than others. This was especially the case for the captains of all the sea vessels who heard the call of duty. They knew what they had to do and acted without hesitation.

[44.] Ibid.

In the words of another volunteer captain of Operation Boatlift, "You forget about what you're supposed to do, what they teach you in school. And you know what, morally, this is the right way to go and deep down this is what I'm going to do."[45] 9/11 was a day when we unified as a collective American tribe—even briefly. While 9/11 was an act that was born out of fear and hatred and one that had the intention to break our national morale, it wound up being a day that witnessed a powerful display of unity and cooperation in the heroism of Operation Boatlift. On that day, none of the boat captains of the various rescue vessels questioned the identity of the throngs of survivors desperately seeking refuge. Passengers coming on board weren't asked: "How much money do you make? What religion do you practice? Where were you born? How do you find love? How do you vote?" These questions were all irrelevant. No one was discriminated against based on religion, status, class, political party, sexuality, or race. On 9/11, we were all members of the same tribe—the human tribe.

Here's why Operation Boatlift exemplifies your capacity for a Happy Brain. The innate human drive to empathize the common suffering of others and the desire to alleviate another's pain and despair is Spiritual Compassion. In today's Age of Disconnection, tribe is the crucial key lacking in order for you to claim your Happy Brain. Why is Spiritual Compassion so vital for your and society's ultimate happiness? Without the love and nurturing received from your parents or other adult caregivers, you wouldn't have survived childhood. A life lacking in the caring and concern from your friends and family is one of despair and dismay. A society that values acts of kindness and charity to all its members fosters a Happy Brain for all.

Brain science reveals a powerful finding—compassion and empathy are essential for your Happy Brain to function, just as are blood and oxygen. Spiritual Compassion is what allows humanity to prosper and societies to thrive. As you might surmise, natural selection favored compassion as another behavioral strategy for survival. There resides a complex network in your Social Brain that

---

[45.] Ibid.

affirms why Spiritual Compassion is an essential key for your Happy Brain and is the tactic to diminish society's Disease of Despair. Let's explore this remarkable system wired into your brain.

I Feel Your Pain, Literally

Do you find it curious when you see others smile or simply hear their laughter, you have the sudden urge to do the same? Or how about when you see a spider crawling up someone's arm? Do you instantly get the same creepy feeling as if it were happening to you? I bet every one of you at some point has experienced or observed this peculiar behavior happening in your life.

What I want you to discover in this lesson is this phenomenon is the result of an extraordinary system evolution wired into your brain that developed specifically for you to recognize the behaviors and to interpret the emotions of others. By learning to sense and respond to cues from those in your social environment, this remarkable built-in mechanism in neurobiology—known as the *mirror-neuron system* (MNS)—allows you to feel and experience the pain, joy, sadness, surprise, fear, and love of others as if they were your own. This is the brain science behind Spiritual Compassion.

In the context of evolutionary psychology and social behavior, your brain's MNS is a neural mechanism that enriches your Happy Brain. Why so? It has to do with the pro-social feature of compassion that's evidenced throughout human behavior. Spiritual Compassion is an evolutionary strategy based on empathy—the bedrock of any society and the basis of tribe. It's the universal recognition of our common human fragility and frailties. Knowing how your tribe genuinely cares about your well-being is a form of happiness most valuable in your life. Spiritual Compassion is what got you to survive and the tribe to thrive.

Pro-social behaviors such as compassion, empathy, altruism, and perhaps even morality appear to be attributed to this powerful mechanism of your Social Brain—the mirror-neuron system (MNS). As University of Chicago's cognitive neuroscientist Cacioppo proclaims, "[This system] functions to give the observing individual knowledge of the observed action from a 'personal' perspective. This 'personal' understanding of other's actions, it appears, promotes our understanding of and resonance with others. It also accounts for the ways in which merely observing can give rise to a sense of shared fate."[46]

So that spider you just saw crawling up your friend's arm, your Social Brain experiences it as if a spider were actually crawling up your arm. Yikes. The overwhelming feeling of pride you get from watching your kid hit her final scoring homerun lights up the same region of your Social Brain as if you did it. Yeah.

There exists, however, an important element regarding human behavior that may come as a surprise to many of you. Contrary to what you may read in the media or see in the world, humans are more strongly wired for compassion and kindness than for competition and conflict. This phenomenon even applies to many other species. The ability for mammals—including humans—to cooperate and empathize was a powerful observation the famous biologist Charles Darwin witnessed in nature that became the foundation for his noted theories of natural selection, behavior, and—most importantly—the evolution of emotion. Let's face it, humanity would never have made it this far if people didn't rally in times of tragedy or strife. Spiritual Compassion is wired into your Social Brain for a reason—for the human species to survive, for the tribe to thrive.

The complex network of mirror neurons appears to be another strategy for your Social Brain that allows for you to feel what it's proverbially like to "walk in someone else's shoes." The next time you catch yourself crying while watching a tear-jerker film, rejoicing when you hear some uplifting news, or wincing when you witness your favorite sports star getting injured and buckling in pain, your MNS is optimally working. Even if you're only observing the action or merely picturing the event by reading or hearing about it, the same neurons in your Social Brain fire as if you were having that experience

---

[46] John T Cacioppo and William Patrick, *Loneliness: Human Nature and the Need for Social Connection* (W.W. Norton & Company, New York, 2008), pp.154–5.

yourself. Your healthy Social Brain evolved to mirror the actions of what it senses others doing in the world. Why would evolution have your brain do this?

Mirror neurons developed in your Social Brain for one crucial function—as a built-in response to allow you to feel another person's joy, sadness, exuberance, or grief as if it were your own. The MNS enhances your ability to experience empathy toward others—even complete strangers. When you observe someone on the street fall and spill an entire grocery bag of food, your first reaction is to go and help. When you hear a lost child crying at the airport, your MNS gets triggered for you to respond to his cries of panic. Even mentally processing the story about my own grief over losing Mom to suicide might have caused your MNS to fire. Why does this happen? What would be the evolutionary advantage behind this feature of neurobiology?

Your Social Brain suffers when it knows others are suffering; you cringe when recognizing others are in pain. To encourage that you'll come to the aid and assistance to those in your tribe in times of crisis, the MNS activates the same region of your own brain as the actual areas in the brains of other people. It's due to your brain's MNS that accounts for the numerous acts of altruism and courage on 9/11 and the success behind Operation Boatlift.

On an annoying note, your brain's MNS also activates in other situations in life, such as the love for gossiping, or—my pet peeve—rubber-necking. It's the reason you find drivers slowing down to observe an accident on the side of the road. It's your Social Brain's default mode for empathy that's behind the phenomenon of rubber-necking. While some might regard the action as a nuisance, the instinctive drive for your Social Brain to be curious and be concerned is what makes you slow down your car and turn your neck. Evolution primed your Social Brain to assess if anyone's hurt. It's the same reason you instinctively yell "Fire!" and place an emergency call when you see smoke and flames come out of a building. In all these cases, your MNS is properly functioning.

This remarkable aspect of human behavior is yet another convincing piece of evidence to suggest how your brain fundamentally evolved into a social organ. Your Social Brain is constantly mirroring whatever actions you observe and emotions you register in your social milieu. While it appears indisputable the MNS exists as part of human biology, the more puzzling question is its function for humanity's development in the first place. Here's one possible explanation.

Prior to the invention of verbal language, humans were limited to communicate non-verbally. Before early humans could express their thoughts and feelings through words, they had to rely on facial gestures, body language, and social cues. Even today, parents are limited to gauge their infant's needs based solely on his or her cries and body expressions. In the most basic sense, your MNS is the "monkey see monkey do" mechanism of your Social Brain that allowed for early humans to "mirror" the actions and behaviors of others to know what they're feeling, sensing, and thinking before humans mastered verbal language. But just to be clear, your MNS functions well beyond just vision, as your other senses of taste, smell, hearing, and touch equally and powerfully are regulated by your brain's MNS.

Your MNS substantiates that "[s]ocial interaction is an essential part of being human. Some believe that we are born with an innate desire and ability for social interaction. The intrinsic necessity for social interaction has been suggested as evolution's motivating factor for uniquely human skills including art, language, theory of mind and empathy. One system proposed to underlie many aspects of social cognition is the mirror neuron system (MNS)."[47] To put this another way, your brain's MNS allows you to experience what is technically called an "empathic response," a term you can think of as "being on the same emotional and social page" with others.

Empathy is the invisible hand that diminishes the Disease of Despair and generates Spiritual Compassion in your life and in the world. Practicing compassion and extending empathy to others are

---

[47.] Lindsay M. Oberman, Jaime A. Pineda, and Vilayanur S. Ramachandran, "The human mirror neuron system: A link between action observation and social skills," SCAN (2007) 2, 62.

yet another way for you to achieve a Happy Brain. You might find it interesting to know how the words *compassion* and *empathy* respectively derive from the Latin *com-passio* and the Ancient Greek *em-patheia* that mean "to be in the state of suffering with." Compassion and empathy enable you to be united in and to experience the shared suffering, anguish, pain, and struggles of others.

Your MNS interacts in a way that integrates compassion and your Happy Brain, exemplified by the following equation:

$$\text{Compassion} = \text{Social Brain} = \text{Happy Brain}$$
$$\text{Callousness} = \text{Solitary Brain} = \text{Despairing Brain}$$

The degree to which you're capable of extending Spiritual Compassion for others—even complete strangers—is the key for your Happy Brain. When you opt to operate out of kindness and compassion—instead of apathy and callousness—you minimize the suffering of those around you, including yourself. Essentially, if you want to ensure your own happiness, it's also important to focus on the happiness of others.

Compassion Creates Your Happy Brain

While it might not be obvious on the surface, humans are fundamentally driven by compassion, empathy, and altruism. Just look at 9/11, Hurricane Harvey, the horrific Pittsburgh synagogue shootings, and what happens in the aftermath of these and other monumental calamities. Although it's true these situations can certainly illicit fear and see some of you revert to your base primal needs for survival, they yield to your deep sense of community and your commitment to rushing to aid others—even complete strangers.

Here's a truism that's largely forgotten and urgently in need to remember in today's Age of Disconnection: *We love more than we hate. We care more than we are cruel.* Spiritual Compassion is the solution to eradicate the Disease of Despair and promote your Happy Brain. It manifests in your life when you can learn to extend Spiritual

Compassion to those beyond your immediate tribe—beyond your friends and family. Yet this is precisely what the last Happiness Hijack prevents from occurring: *Happiness is extending empathy to only those in your tribe.*

One of the greatest perils on the rise in today's world is the negative aspect of tribe—*tribalism.* When you only limit your compassion and altruism to those you consider to be "in your tribe," it will ultimately sabotage your Happy Brain. Here's the important distinction I want you to know between the positive attributes of tribe and negative qualities of tribalism. Tribe is the optimal expression of your Social Brain that's geared toward community, connection, and cooperation. On the other hand, tribalism is the primal expression of your Stone-Age Tribe brain that operates through the lens of strife, scarcity, and suspicion. To be more succinct—your Social Brain favors tribe; your Stone-Age Tribe brain focuses on tribalism.

Every one of you has the potential for extending empathy and compassion toward others—even those you might view to be "outside your tribe." It happened on 9/11. Society's challenge is being able to operate from the collective Social Brain's unconditional capacity for empathy and compassion outside of crisis situations and calamities, while not remaining locked in the Stone-Age Tribe brain's drive of "conditional compassion." The Spiritual Strategy of Compassion makes that possible, but it takes practice.

Brain science exposes how compassion is a natural feature of human neurobiology, as evidenced by the MNS. It's the long thread of compassion that sews the tapestry of humanity. To paraphrase the words of Harvard biologist Martin Nowak—the hallmark of the human species *isn't the struggle for survival, but the snuggle for survival.*

As altruism researcher, Post, states, "The idea that human beings are inclined towards helpful prosocial and altruistic behavior seems incontrovertible, and it is highly plausible that the inhibition of such behavior and related emotions would be unhealthy... Perhaps those of us in contemporary technological cultures are isolated in various respects and have strayed too far from our altruistic proclivities."[48]

The key to humanity's survival and the future of the human race may well reside in the complex network of your brain's mirror-neuron system and the innate human ability to cultivate compassion for others. Social apathy—a dangerous impediment to Spiritual Compassion—is a product of your malnourished Social Brain that lacks Vitamin S and what accelerates the Disease of Despair. The more social apathy there exists in the world, the more anger, anxiety, and addiction grip society. Acquiring the ability to engender Spiritual Compassion and express empathy is the glue that binds the tribe and what advances your Happy Brain. This is how I came to value Spiritual Compassion in my own life.

After the third day of Mom's suicide attempt, she still remained in a comatose state. Based on the severity of her medical condition, the prognosis from her doctors concluded how Mom would unlikely ever emerge from her coma—and even if she did, there was irreparable damage to her brain, due to the elapsed time it took from attempting suicide to getting her to the emergency room. Knowing Mom's condition was beyond any chance of a full recovery, my father, brother, and I were left with one of the hardest decisions we've ever had to make—whether to leave Mom in that comatose state for the rest of her life or to act out of mercy and terminate her life support.

Unarguably, it was the most agonizing conversation I'll likely ever have in my entire life. In the span of fifteen minutes, I felt an array of emotions ranging from anger, fear, guilt, despair, panic, horror, and hopelessness. It's a loathsome situation that I wish none of you ever will endure in your lifetime. Ultimately, it was agreed by the three of us how the best course of action was to end Mom's suffering. Fortunately for us, the ethical decision to follow through with this act was one legally stipulated in Mom's will and testament as her medical request. Despite the misgivings what others outside of the immediate family might have felt at the time, I remember to

---

[48] Steven Post, "Altruism, Happiness, and Health: It's Good to Be Good," *International Journal of Behavioral Medicine* 2005, Vol. 12, No. 2, 71.

this day the tremendous amount of solidarity from everyone there the moment we arrived at this heart-breaking decision. Having that unwavering show of sympathy and strength from everyone when we decided to discontinue Mom's life-support was priceless. It exemplified the testament of Spiritual Compassion that comes from being part of an empathetic and embracing tribe that loves you unconditionally.

Spiritual Compassion remains potent for another reason. The human emotions of love and empathy are concepts imparted by all the world's religions and taught by spiritual teachers. It's only recently that science—specifically brain science and behavioral health—indicates why expressing compassion and acting altruistically are another evolutionary advantage that favors human survival. You instinctively come to the aid of others in moments of pain and panic, in times of strife and stress. You equally rejoice in times of abundance and happiness of others. It's what accounts for the heroism behind Operation Boatlift.

A poignant and universal example how compassion and altruism are found among all cultures, religions, and societies is the Golden Rule—the spiritual equivalent of the science of altruism and the neurobiology behind compassion. Variations of the Golden Rule are evident in all the major world's religions. Here are a few examples—of course there are certainly many more to be found in other traditions and cultures.

1) **Christianity**—Jesus: "Do to others what you would want them to do to you." (Luke 6:31)
2) **Islam**—Mohammed: "That which you want for yourself, seek for mankind."
3) **Judaism**—"You shall not take vengeance or bear a grudge against your kinsfolk. Love your neighbor as yourself." (Leviticus: 19:18)
4) **Buddhism**—Buddha: "Hurt not others in ways that you yourself would find hurtful." (Udana-Varga, 5:18)

5) **Hinduism**—"This is the sum of Dharma [duty]: Do naught unto others which would cause you pain if done to you." (Mahabharata, 5:1517)

6) **Jainism**—Mahavira: "In happiness and suffering, in joy and grief, we should regard all creatures as we regard our own self." (*24th Tirthankara*)

7) **Sikhism**—"Don't create enmity with anyone as God is within everyone." (Guru Arjan Devji 259)

8) **Confucianism**—"What you do not wish for yourself, do not do to others." (Confucius)

What's one easy and powerful way for you to revel in a Happy Brain? By learning to embody the Golden Rule into your everyday life—from the homeless person on the street to your neighbors. The Golden Rule is a valuable reminder how every one of you wants to be treated with dignity, respect, and—most of all—with kindness and compassion. The Golden Rule is another dynamic example in which science and spirituality align to advance the same message—compassion is a human behavior deeply valued by all. Regularly expressing Spiritual Compassion builds your Happy Brain.

Happy Brain Homework

The Happiness course you're taking is more than merely learning about the latest research for achieving your Happy Brain; it's about applying the tools for happiness into your life. Here's the "Acting on Happiness" exercise you might enjoy trying. Assuming you have the time and the means, is there something you can do—beyond than just donating money to a charity or a cause—that advances more kindness and compassion in your community? Can you volunteer a few hours of your weekend working at a local food bank, visiting the elderly at a retirement community, or reading to kids at the public library?

Even if you don't have the luxury of time or ability to engage in service work, starting tomorrow I want you to commit performing some simple, random acts of kindness. Here are some examples of how that might look. The next time you find yourself driving in rush-hour traffic and a car is trying to merge into your lane, instead of getting angry and honking your horn, be kind and let the other driver pass. Say "hello" and "thank you" the next time you see the person who delivers your mail or transports packages to and from your office. When you're at the grocery store and you notice someone has callously left a shopping cart in the middle of the parking lot, return it to the proper place so it doesn't take up an empty parking space for someone else to use. Smile to at least five people you pass by on the street every day. Of course, you can be creative and think of many more acts of altruism to help build your Happy Brain.

It's been long known how benevolent behaviors have positive effects on the health and well-being of the recipient. As Post recounts, "[I]t points to the now widely accepted biopsychosocial model that being loved, cared for, and supported by others is critically important to health and treatment efficacy."[49] But there's something even more amazing about performing acts of kindness. What's only been revealed recently in studies is how such acts of compassion and kindness equally impact the agents—the one performing these actions. That means you!

As ongoing brain science research suggests, the likely reason for this phenomenon can be explained back to your brain's mirror-neuron system. It appears your MNS switches on when you observe how your acts of kindness positively benefit the recipient. In turn, acting out of compassion co-activates your own feelings of contentment and joy when acknowledging the good deeds that you just did. But the benefits from your acts of kindness don't just stop with you; they have a ripple effect onto the world. The person who directly benefits from your kindness is even more likely than before to do something nice for someone else—generally within the next hour. Furthermore, just witnessing your acts of kindness can cause others to be more empathetic and caring throughout their day.

---

49. Ibid., 67.

Spiritual Compassion generates a "wavelength of happiness" for both you and the recipient of your kindness. It's literally a win-win for you, others, and the world. It achieves this by fostering social solidarity and social resilience among the tribe. As Post continues to convey, "Altruism results in deeper and more positive social integration, distraction from personal problems and the anxiety of self-preoccupation, enhanced meaning and purpose as related to well-being, a more active lifestyle that counters cultural pressures toward isolated passivity, and the presence of positive emotions such as kindness that displace harmful negative emotional states."[50]

Science now provides a cogent reason why you actually achieve a Happy Brain when you engender empathy and convey compassion to others. Why do I know you'll experience a sense of contentment when acting altruistically and extending kindness to others? Your Social Brain will reward you with genuine feelings of happiness. In a nutshell, *you feel good when doing good for others.*

Bonus Content

- Visit www.ScienceofaHappyBrain.com and discover more ways to apply the Happiness Strategy of Compassion to build your Happy Brain.
- Enjoy the full video of Operation BoatLift.
- Engage in and share how your own "Acting on Happiness" stories boost your Happy Brain at www.ScienceofaHappyBrain.com.

---

50. Ibid., 70.

LESSON TEN

HAPPY BRAINS MAKE
A HAPPY WORLD

> If civilization is to survive, we must cultivate
> the science of human relationships—the ability
> of all peoples, of all kinds, to live together, in the
> same world at peace.
>
> —Franklin D. Roosevelt

Your Happy Brain

Congratulations on completing your Happiness course. You've done an amazing job acquiring many valuable insights and applying strategies from brain science and spirituality on what happiness is and ways for you to enjoy the benefits of a Happy Brain. For your last lesson let's summarize the main points you've learned throughout your Happiness course. I also want to make the case why developing your Happy Brain is the key to balance, longevity, and resilience. You'll also explore how your Happy Brain makes a happy world.

But before doing so, do you remember the very first exercise I had you do in the opening lesson—defining what happiness means to you? Having mastered the concepts and engaged with exercises throughout the previous lessons, are you curious to see if your understanding of happiness has changed? If you opted to write your happiness letter by hand, you're welcome to do the same here. If you

175

originally composed it online, go to www.ScienceofaHappyBrain.
com to begin this exercise. I now wish for you to answer thoughtfully
and in detail these important questions. Feel free to take your time
when answering and please be sure not to refer to your original letter.
Here are the questions for this final exercise in your Happiness course:

1) Having explored the various ways my happiness can be
   hijacked, what does an ideal life of happiness currently
   look like to me?
2) What valuable insights have I acquired for advancing my
   Happy Brain?
3) Based on the tools I've now learned, is there a specific
   happiness strategy I can start today to implement into my
   life? Describe how that will happen.
4) Was there an issue standing in the way of my personal
   happiness when I wrote the original letter? Do I have a
   better perspective in resolving or dealing with this issue? If
   so, explain how?

Once you've finished your final exercise, I invite you to open
your sealed envelope or follow the instructions you received to access
your online version and read your original happiness letter. Has your
definition of happiness remained the same, or are you surprised to
learn how your outlook on happiness has evolved? Most people report
the latter. Let's explore the possible explanations for why that's the
case by summarizing the main points from your Happiness course.

One very important point advanced at the start of your
Happiness course is how the Declaration of Independence rightfully
states the "pursuit of Happiness" is exactly that—a pursuit. Happiness
doesn't come to you naturally. Happiness is something you have to
pursue with practice and perseverance. If you recall the important
point from the first lesson: "*It's not the promise of happiness, it's the
practice of happiness.*" It's precisely what research in brain science
and wisdom from spiritual traditions affirm. Achieving your Happy
Brain takes practice.

Nature doesn't give a hoot about your happiness. Evolution didn't wire your brain to be happy; it wired your brain to survive. Evolution achieved this goal in a very cunning way by making your brain become averse to pain and addicted to pleasure. Think of pain and pleasure as the opposite ends of the Survival Spectrum. Human behavior is forever fluctuating between these two terminal points of the Survival Spectrum, thus hijacking your happiness.

On one end of the Survival Spectrum, your brain's stress-response system alerts you to painful situations and experiences that threaten homeostasis. Thus, your brain is wired to avoid pain. On the other end of the Survival Spectrum, your brain's dopaminergic-reward system entices you to pleasurable situations and experiences that entreat homeostasis. The sensation of pain is the way for an organism to know it's out of homeostasis—the state of balance for optimal functioning. The sensation of pleasure became a strategy for humans to be motivated to perpetuate actions and behaviors that enhance survival. Here's the takeaway: Pain is a threat for your brain; pleasure is a treat for your brain.

While pain and pleasure became effective strategies for survival, they sabotage your quest for a Happy Brain. Think of pain and pleasure as evolutionary relics of your Stone-Age Tribe brain. Again, recall the exercises outlined in the first few lessons that underscore how your Stone-Age Tribe brain views life via the lens of strife, scarcity, and suspicion. As a result, your Stone-Age Tribe brain is singularly focused on survival and self-preservation. Pain is a signal to your brain that there exist threats to your survival. Pleasure is a way for your brain to be rewarded for actions that promote survival.

That said, one key strategy for your Stone-Age ancestors was the realization how banding into tribes—for promoting safety, security, and stability—became an adaptive behavior that favored survival of the species. Just as humans developed opposable thumbs—along with the anatomy for walking upright, running, and human language—tribe was another powerful evolutionary strategy for human survival. As a result, this core aspect of human neurobiology and behavior became the basis for the Social Brain system.

It's your Social Brain that holds the secret and is the unrecognized strategy for achieving your Happy Brain. More research in brain science continues to attest how your brain complexified and fundamentally developed as a social organ. Various systems and mechanisms developed in your brain over the course of millennia to reinforce the innate human drive for community and connection.

One revolutionary finding provides credence to this notion: shared regions of your brain process and co-regulate social pain as physical pain. The strategy behind this "piggybacking" of the response to social pain with overlapping regions that experience physical pain is how your Social Brain alerts you to threats of social stress in your environment. The ability for "pain to feel all the same to your brain" is nature's strategy for survival of the species. Pain and distress in any form force you to seek out the safety and support from others—your tribe.

From whichever perspective you choose to view it, one fact remains: Nature shaped your Social Brain as a powerful, adaptive strategy that secured the survival of the human species. This undeniable, shared aspect of humanity remains the fundamental reason why—even today—every one of you necessitates attachment to tribe. Yet, living in an Age of Disconnection makes you crave community and belonging more than ever. One central concept of your Happiness course is how the lack of tribe in today's world has become the driving force behind the rise in the Disease of Despair—precipitated from our Age of Disconnection—that is wreaking havoc in society. The Disease of Despair manifests as the dangerously accelerating rates of suicide, depression, chronic anxiety, addiction, mental disease, and behavioral disorders rampant today. As a result, more of you are at risk of going against what thousands of years of human evolution bred you for and what nature programmed you to do—to tribe.

But something very scary and sinister is occurring in today's world. The functional strategy that was once the primary tactic for humanity's survival—the need for tribe—is becoming distorted and artificially augmented by technology that miserably fails to become a viable and nurturing substitute for your Social Brain.

The hazards from society's Age of Disconnection is scrambling your Social Brain and compounding the Disease of Despair. There exists an entire generation being starved from social nourishment in the form of Vitamin S and growing up unknowingly infected by the illness of isolation. Vast segments of society are gripped by the Disease of Despair, resulting in your despairing brain and a society in desperation. In just the past few decades, society has morphed into one that dangerously continues to malnourish your Social Brain. Living in a time that plummets deeper into the Disease of Despair, you risk becoming more socially disconnected and disengaged from others. It's necessary to add in another line into the original Happiness Equation to reflect this crisis unfolding in today's world.

Attachment to Tribe = Life = Happy Brain
Abandonment from Tribe = Death = Despairing Brain
Annihilation of Tribe = Extinction = Dysfunctional Society

Not only are more individuals feeling abandonment from the tribe; it's the horror how there's been a gradual annihilation of the importance of and ability for tribe in today's technologically modern world and virtual lifestyle. It's this equation that simultaneously represents the sabotage and solution behind your malnourished Social Brain and the perils of the Disease of Despair that affects us individually and collectively. It's a simple and powerful rubric that's often ignored when attempting to deal with the complex gamut of social, behavioral, political, and health crises due to living in a chaotic and confusing world.

The next big plague to threaten humanity doesn't have to be just biological; it can be socio-technological. The Disease of Despair spreads by living in a 24/7 virtual world of the internet, video games, and augmented reality that can leave you feeling a void on the inside. It's a dangerous sign of humanity's Age of Disconnection when a technologically advanced country like South Korea reports that one in ten teenagers in that country suffers from internet addiction and spends up to eighty-eight hours a week playing online video games.[51]

There was a time when forced social isolation and solitary confinement were used as forms of punishment, due to the cruelty it inflicted on one's psyche and morale. Today, we willingly choose to self-isolate and socially disconnect from being imprisoned behind screens, hijacked by social media, or masked as virtual avatars in video games. The world's twenty-first century fast-paced technologically accelerating Age of Disconnection can make you feel further isolated, desperate, and alone. The result? Your dangerously debilitated Social Brain and a society crippled by the Disease of Despair are generating an epic social, health, and behavioral crisis. Unless society acts swiftly, millions of more people will be at risk.

Humanity urgently requires a new strategy for achieving your Happy Brain, which produces happy people and a happy world. Tribe in the form of rebuilding community, reconnecting in real-time, and remembering how humans originally evolved to socialize is the key for your Happy Brain and a happy world. *Now more than ever, everyone needs tribe.*

Tribe Creates Balance, Longevity, and Resilience

Science verifies how your Social Brain evolved to make you a *human being*, but spirituality reminds you of the importance of *being human*. Both science and spirituality converge to reveal today a tremendous and timeless truth—balance, longevity, and resilience are the rewards of your Happy Brain that are forged the more you nourish your Social Brain and experience attachment to your tribe.

Religion and spirituality have always taught why community and tribe are an integral part of the human experience and vital for your inner peace and society's well-being. Only in the past couple of decades do evolutionary psychology and neurobiology reveal why

---

51. Melia Robinson, "Korea's internet addiction crisis is getting worse, as teens spend up to 88 hours a week gaming," *Business Insider*, Mar. 25, 2015.

your drive for tribe is expressed in your genes and wired into your brain. The emerging model of the Social Brain and of humans having evolved essentially as social creatures is gaining further prominence within various scientific disciplines. It's the powerful ability for socialization and the drive to tribe that appears to be the success story behind humans becoming the predominant species on the planet. What's more alarming is how the lack of tribe and the diminishment of experiencing real-time human interactions compromise your balance, longevity, and resilience in life. Here's why.

Balance—Social disengagement and feelings of loneliness are expressions of the Disease of Despair and the fatal outcome from a society living in an Age of Disconnection. The rise in social media, digital dependence, time spent at work staring at screens, and longer commutes trapped hours daily in cars all result in something far more devastating and damaging to you. You go about your day further experiencing life disconnected in an over-connected world. Brain science reveals how these behaviors—that you can take for granted—disrupt your Social Brain and ultimately sabotage your ability to experience equanimity and stability, as they can prompt you to experience greater anger, anxiety, and addiction in your life.

Just step into the most technologically advanced penthouses or opulent mansions around the world—that exemplify society's epitome of success and achievement—to see the bathroom cabinets of the rich and famous lined with prescription medication to combat stress, anxiety, and depression. It reveals an ugly truth: All the money in the world will never immunize you against the rising epidemic in the Disease of Despair. Status, fame, luxury goods, wealth, and power are what society wants you to believe are the sources for your Happy Brain, but they're no substitute for the peace of mind experienced in knowing you belong to a group that genuinely loves and cares about you. *Tribe nourishes your Social Brain to generate balance in your brain, body, and being.*

Longevity—What studies in social medicine and public policy are increasingly starting to affirm is how non-communicable diseases (NCDs) such as diabetes, alcoholism, suicide, addiction, obesity, heart disease, Alzheimer's disease, and mental illness are all on the rise. The World Health Organization reports that in 2017, NCDs accounted for nearly forty million deaths—that's about 70 percent of all deaths worldwide.[52] As one medical report states, "There is strong evidence that higher levels of social integration are associated with lower morbidity and mortality rates. A recent meta-analysis to determine the extent to which social relationships influence risk for mortality found a fifty percent increased likelihood of survival for participants with stronger social relationships, an influence comparable with the 'lifestyle' risk factors."[53]

Here's another way to say it: *Deaths from non-communicable diseases are due to non-communication.* While it's been known for decades that genetic and behavioral factors contribute to the rise in NCDs, the results from studies like these undeniably state why lack of social connection appears to be one of the leading components that place people at risk of dying from an NCD. As one study affirms, "One of the most robust social risk factors involves the number and quality of an individual's close personal relationships. People who are socially isolated have increased risk of death from all causes, and several specific infectious, cancerous, and cardiovascular diseases."[54] *Tribe is the key for your fortified Social Brain that increases longevity in your brain, body, and being.*

Resilience—More health practitioners realize the perils from social isolation and feelings of loneliness. They declare how advancing social networks—not just on social media—is what builds your resilient brain and a robust society. Your malnourished Social Brain weakens your body's immune system and dysregulates your nervous system by putting your brain, body, and being under stress. Chronic stress in the form of social isolation triggers your body's inflammation that, in turn, makes you more susceptible to physical disease, a shorter life span, and mental illness.

---

52. Wendy Holmes and Jennifer Joseph, "Social participation and healthy ageing: a neglected, significant protective factor for chronic non-communicable conditions," *Globalization and Health*, 2011,7, 43.

53. Ibid.

54. Jane Collingwood, "Study Probes How Emotions Affect Immune System," *PsychCentral*, May 2014.

Research in behavioral medicine, social health, and public policy correlate how your atrophied Social Brain suppresses society's social networks and fractures our health-care paradigm. What does it mean? *Your strongly developed Social Brain results from being part of a tribe that brings resilience in your brain, body, and being.*

All the research appears to point to one powerful and undeniable truth—learning the tools for achieving balance, longevity, and resilience combats the rising tide of anger, anxiety, and addiction, all of which is enhanced by interaction with your tribe. Tribe is the timeless strategy required for your Happy Brain. This strategy is grounded in the emerging Bio-Psycho-Socio-Spiritual model of your Happy Brain that directly relates to the four Happiness Strategies of Comfort, Contribution, Connection, and Compassion. Let's recap what these are.

Biological Comfort—Lesson Six recounts how the Biological Strategy of Comfort manifests within the tribe of parents "united by grief" from the death of a child. While Cara may never be able to reclaim the happiness she once enjoyed, there exists comfort in knowing her grief is seen, heard, and witnessed authentically by those in this community helping her in some small way to cope with her trauma. In the absence of tribe, your Social Brain dysregulates and experiences "separation anxiety disorder"—a prevalent symptom in today's Age of Disconnection that tends to exacerbate society's anger, anxiety, and addiction.

Your Social Brain evolved a remarkable ability for you to regulate pain in times of crisis and conflict, known as the Brain's Opioid Theory of Social Attachment (BOTSA). From the perspective of evolutionary psychology, the Happiness Hijack of defining happiness as the avoidance and aversion from pain can undermine your Happy Brain. Learning to accept the support from your tribe in times of pain and grief generates your Happy Brain that can overcome the Happiness Hijack of wanting to avoid or mask pain. The Biological Comfort you receive from your tribe brings safety, security, and stability in your life. *Comfort is the Biological Strategy for your Happy Brain.*

Psychological Contribution—Lesson Seven reveals the Psychological Strategy of Contribution, illustrated by the transformational story of Drake's decision to join—and eventually to leave—the violent Crips gang. What Drake tragically endured in his early childhood was a form of abandonment from tribe witnessed by the lack of the three primal drives for feeling value, belonging, and engagement to a tribe. Drake was desperately seeking one thing he was missing in life—the need to be needed. Homeostasis—the state of equilibrium for an organism to experience optimal functioning—is required for your Happy Brain. Your body's stress-response system, governed by the HPA-axis and the ANS, goes into a heightened state of dysregulation whenever changes in your environment disrupt homeostasis. Stress, in whatever form, triggers your body's inflammation response that can negatively impact your Happy Brain.

As a gang member, Drake's deeper and primal craving for feeling needed and valued was a powerful motivation not to leave his Crips tribe. Why? Although he felt security, his life deeply lacked Psychological Contribution, which manifests as the second Happiness Hijack for never being satisfied in the present. For Drake, not being able to find enduring satisfaction in the present moment as a Crips gang member sabotaged his Happy Brain. Knowing and living out your purpose in life act as an antidote for the Disease of Despair. Leading a meaningful life nourishes your Happy Brain and is one powerful strategy to diminish your exposure to anger, anxiety, and addiction. For Drake, his Happy Brain comes from the Psychological Contribution in knowing how his life actively benefits the greater world by dedicating his life in service as an addiction counselor for at-risk youth. *Contribution is the Psychological Strategy for your Happy Brain.*

Social Connection—Lesson Eight tells the heart-wrenching story of Wanda, who in the grips of social isolation and deep feelings of loneliness, wrote a desperate plea for social contact to her neighbors. Her tragic situation exposes how vulnerable you can become from living in a society that normalizes psychological individualism and social isolationism, as they greatly weaken your Social Brain. Wanda's search for Social Connection provides a salient reminder how your brain evolved as a social organ and requires regular doses of Vitamin S in the form of tribe for building your Happy Brain. More so than anti-depressants, the therapy Wanda and her Social Brain craved most is a form of "social medicine" in knowing she belongs to a tribe. Your Stone-Age Tribe brain's drive for survival is the neurobiological explanation behind the experience of pleasure. It's the same reason why food, sex, and sleep are so enjoyable—they're all functional strategies that are pleasurable and increase the odds for humans to persevere.

The dopaminergic-reward system regulates your motivation and governs the anticipatory reward networks in your brain. The reward of pleasure became the evolutionary motivation for you to continue actions, despite their challenges. This phenomenon accounts for why there exists a shared region of your brain that gets triggered when you crave both food and friendship. Your brain associates the primal pleasure of socialization for survival just as powerfully for food as sustenance. Another sabotage for your Happy Brain is the Happiness Hijack that states how happiness is exclusively an individual pursuit and not a collective one. Despite having thousands of followers on Instagram and an active social media profile, authentic Social Connection is what satiates your Social Brain and is another tactic for your Happy Brain. *Connection is the Social Strategy for your Ha7ppy Brain.*

Spiritual Compassion—Lesson Nine commemorates the heroic actions of Operation Boatlift, in which hundreds of sea vessels converged onto Lower Manhattan to rescue thousands of frightened victims on 9/11. The heroism and bravery witnessed on that day by Captains Ardolino, Jones, and countless others exemplified the universal power of tribe. Learning how to empathize over the welfare and well-being of others, whether those close to you or complete strangers is a hallmark of your Social Brain. Spiritual Compassion is taught by all the world's religions and is most needed to combat the Disease of Despair. It's the compassion and caring exchanged between you and others that create your Happy Brain.

The complex network of neurons that allows you to associate and attune to the emotional and social cues of others is the brain's mirror-neuron system (MNS). Your Social Brain's MNS evolved for one crucial function—for you to feel another person's emotions and experiences, as if they were your own. Believing how happiness comes from only extending empathy to those in your tribe is another Happiness Hijack for your Happy Brain. The cognitive "us versus them" frame of life isn't an expression of tribe; it's the product of tribalism. Spiritual Compassion that manifests as the empathy and altruism over the safety and security of others—even complete strangers—is another foundation for your Happy Brain. This is a timeless truth society has forgotten and why Operation Boatlift is a perfect reflection of humanity operating at its best—as a tribe. *Compassion is the Spiritual Strategy for your Happy Brain.*

Biological Comfort, Psychological Contribution, Social Connection, and Spiritual Compassion exemplify various systems and neural networks in your brain that reinforce pro-social behaviors and that substantiate the Social Brain model of human development. The following table summarizes these key points.

Table 3.

ELEMENT OF HAPPY BRAIN	STRATEGY FOR HAPPY BRAIN	SYSTEM IN HAPPY BRAIN	EXPERIENCE OF HAPPY BRAIN
BIOLOGICAL	COMFORT	BRAIN'S OPIOID THEORY OF SOCIAL ATTACHMENT (BOTSA)	HAPPINESS IS COMFORT FROM YOUR TRIBE
PSYCHO-LOGICAL	CONTRI-BUTION	STRESS AND INFLAMMATION RESPONSE SYSTEM	HAPPINESS IS CONTRIBUTION FOR YOUR TRIBE
SOCIAL	CONNECTION	DOPAMINERGIC-REWARD SYSTEM	HAPPINESS IS CONNECTION WITH YOUR TRIBE
SPIRITUAL	COMPASSION	MIRROR-NEURON SYSTEM ((MNS)	HAPPINESS IS COMPASSION FOR THOSE OUTSIDE YOUR TRIBE

Looking Forward into the Past

The real-life stories of Cara, Drake, Wanda, and Operation Boatlift express the core aspect of the human condition that associates attachment to your tribe as survival and your Happy Brain, while abandonment from your tribe as death and your despairing brain. Banding into tribes became an evolutionary tactic for your early ancestors. Early humans who recognized the adaptive advantage and mastered the functional strategy of forming into tribes passed on that behavioral trait into the DNA of you and to every human alive today. Tribe, your Social Brain, and your Happy Brain are intertwined.

The future of society hangs on tribe—literally. The power of tribe is the unbroken thread that weaves the past into the present and what extends humanity into the future. We're living in a pivotal moment in human history—one that has unwittingly turned humanity's Age of Digitalization into the Age of Disconnection. It's the sad state from today's Age of Disconnection that's accelerating the age of anger, anxiety, and addiction. Modern society has forgotten something fundamentally true—you're more *Homo Socialis* than you're *Homo Sapiens*. You're more a "social human" than you're a "wise human."

Tribe is a universal archetype of the human psyche. Just as the human qualities of love, death, good, and evil are universal themes expressed through all periods and people, tribe is a timeless trope that's embedded into the very fabric of humanity's collective consciousness. Regardless of your race, politics, religion, class, gender, sexuality, or culture, it's the elemental archetype of tribe that unites humanity. It's the reason that makes you strongly long for tribe in a world grasping for meaning, thirsting for connection, and seeking happiness. Tribe is the link between your Social Brain and your Happy Brain. Here's one final equation that summarizes these points.

Social Brain = Tribe = Happy Brain
Solitary Brain = Lack of Tribe = Despairing Brain

The instinct to tribe runs deep in your blood and resides deep in your brain. Your primal drive for food, sex, and shelter bears equal importance as your intrinsic need for feeling value, belonging, and engagement in the world. Humanity's greatest success story resides in our superior ability to create social bonds, therefore, forming social tribes. It's easy to forget that despite tremendous advances in technology and human achievements to modernize, you're essentially a social being—you crave connection, you seek community, and you desperately long for attachment to your tribe, all of which have become more endangered in modern society.

As Lieberman aptly states,

> The great double-edged sword of being the most sophisticated mammals on the planet is that no matter how smart or rational we become, we can't outthink our basic needs. We all need people to love and respect, and we all need people who love and respect us. Would life without them be worth it?... Those basic social needs are present at birth to ensure our survival, but we are guided by these needs until the end of our days. We do not always recognize these needs, and we may not see them influencing those around us, but they are still there nonetheless.[55]

Any attempt to get rid of your Social Brain—including your primal Stone-Age Tribe brain—would be like trying to live without your respiratory or circulatory system. All of these systems are indelibly imprinted into your brain and programmed into your behavior, as an evolutionary strategy for survival, that they've become instinctive. Any endeavor to eliminate tribe from your life would be equally as deadly for you. Tribe—like your biological necessity to breathe and your dependency on food—is a primal feature wired into your

---

[55.] Lieberman, *Social*, 299.

neurobiology. Without breath or blood, you die. Without tribe, humanity dies.

Science continues to discover and affirm the Bio-Psycho-Socio-Spiritual model and its key to claiming your Happy Brain, along with the long-term survival of humanity. While evolution primed humans to tribe as a means to enhance survival, our challenge today as a species is to leverage the power of tribe as a strategy for our future. Tribe is the overarching winning tactic linking humanity's past, present, and future. Tribe co-regulates your Social Brain and your Happy Brain. Tribe is your antidote for thriving in the age of anger, anxiety, and addiction and the key for creating your Happy Brain and happy world.

One of the biggest threats today and to the future of humanity is the perpetuation of tribalism—the cognitive "us versus them" frame of life—that has become an evolutionary holdover from your Stone-Age Tribe brain. Similarly, the most significant challenge society faces is to express the same positive aspects of tribe that manifest during these times of crisis and learning how to apply the power of tribe all the time—in both the good and bad, during chaos and calm.

Operating out of tribalism—the "us versus them" attitude so pervasive today—is the root cause behind racism, enmity, and social injustice in the world that can further accelerate the dangers of anger, anxiety, and addiction. The political, social, cultural, and ideological upheaval erupting around the world is the negative consequence of humanity collectively operating out of the Stone-Age Tribe brain. It manifests as fear, animosity, and vitriol in society. The more you learn how to function from your Social Brain and the more you're able to tame your Stone-Age Tribe brain, the result is more than just the benefits of your Happy Brain. It's a happy world.

It's the human drive for cooperation and collaboration, for altruism and attachment, and for compassion and empathy that allowed your Social Brain to come into existence. Yet these very attributes that championed humanity's success are the same elements that are missing in today's Age of Disconnection and that are required to create your Happy Brain and a happy world.

Tribe is the foundation for healing both you and the world. Your tribe comes in many names, shapes, and sizes—family, community, neighborhood, fraternity, leagues, congregation, sports teams, workplace, support network, and life-long friends are all powerful expressions of tribe. It doesn't matter how you choose to tribe.

The four Happiness Strategies of Biological Comfort, Psychological Contribution, Social Connection, and Spiritual Compassion become the basis for your Happy Brain that benefits both you and society. Learning to express these four Happiness Strategies on a daily basis generates your Happy Brain, while protecting you from the threats to your health and happiness imposed by the age of anger, anxiety, and addiction. When more of you actively operate out of your Happy Brain, the world becomes a happier place. What unites all four Happiness Strategies is that they're grounded in the Social Brain model. Your brain is a Social Brain. Your Social Brain is the key to your Happy Brain. In actuality, your Social Brain and your Happy Brain are one and the same.

Your Social Brain has more than the ability to create your Happy Brain; it has the power to save humanity. What if the underlying solution sought to address the myriad of social, economic, behavioral, and global crises society is in the midst of has an answer from humanity's shared past—the ability to tribe. Tribe creates your Happy Brain; tribe is the antidote for the age of anger, anxiety, and addiction to secure a happy world.

What Can I Do?

Here's your final lesson in the Happiness course. To what end should you be motivated to achieve a Happy Brain? Well, there's the personal reason, of course. As you've learned throughout the previous lessons, applying the Happiness Strategies of Biological Comfort, Psychological Contribution, Social Connection, and Spiritual Compassion into your life on a daily basis promotes your Happy Brain. But it does more than just promote your Happy Brain. If we truly are to present solutions for the many challenges that society faces, perhaps you can begin by asking yourself: "What can I do to bring about more happiness in the world? What's one action I can take today not only to develop my Happy Brain, but that of others?" Once you develop the tools and techniques for achieving your Happy Brain in your life, I guarantee you will gain the ability to help make the world a happier place.

So how did I come to claim my Happy Brain and what inspired me to become your Happiness Professor? In my mid-twenties, I experienced what undoubtedly was the most traumatic moment of my life. As tragic and painful as Mom's suicide was for me—along with the subsequent anxiety and depression I endured for years after her death—I strongly doubt I would've become the person I am today, who has deeply experienced loss and anguish. It's why I view myself more than just a voice for suicide prevention; I'm a happiness advocate, who's deeply passionate about helping you claim your life of balance, longevity, and resilience. But before I could be of service to you and others, I had to heal myself and reclaim my Happy Brain.

Sometimes it takes a crisis—whether my personal one of Mom's suicide or a collective one such as gun violence, poverty, homelessness, the rise in suicide, or the opioid epidemic—that forces each of you to find the courage and strength to ask the deeper questions: "What brings my life purpose? What brings my life meaning? What brings my life happiness?" Just as I had to ask myself the hard and painful questions in the years after Mom's untimely and unexpected death, it's crucial—if not dire—for you to have the strength and conviction to delve into the difficult and agonizing questions you equally find in your life and in the world today. It's the only way we can begin to create authentic and lasting change for self and society.

I want you to know one powerful truth—each of you has the capacity and the ability to achieve your Happy Brain. Yes, it takes practice, it takes patience, and it takes perseverance. But most of all, I want you to know it's absolutely possible. I know, because it has happened for me. It's only once I was able to achieve my Happy Brain, I could rightfully be of service to and empower you to do the same.

Having said that, it has been a true delight and privilege having you in this Happiness course. I alone don't have the complete answer to the many bigger questions I've just raised, but together, I know we do. There's no one simple, easy fix to the array of issues facing our country and our world, but the first step begins by taking responsibility and accountability for your individual happiness. The newly emerging science of happiness isn't just one for academics, health professionals, or policy-makers, but for all members of society, including one for you.

While governments, schools, religious institutions, social media, corporations, non-profits, communities, and technology all have an integral role in making the world a happier, kinder, and more civil place, it also needs you. There's no one single solution to the many complex issues we face today, but every one of you has a role to play in the story that's being written. The solution resides in all voices within the tribe to be present and heard, for the benefits of a Happy Brain to manifest across the boundaries of politics, race, religion, sexuality, gender, class, and ethnicity.

The discoveries I've made step by step, whether accidentally or intentionally, have all added up to my personal path of awakening. I respectfully welcome your personal experiences and feedback in order to spark a collective conversation. I welcome you to become part of this newly created tribe—one geared around the creation of enduring balance, longevity, and resilience for all. I invite you to share the wisdom you've now acquired with others in your tribe. Tell, gift, or share with at least five people you know about *Science of a Happy Brain*.

I certainly never envisioned nor planned for this to be my life's purpose, but I fell into it while on my personal road of transformation and discovery. At times the road ahead can seem daunting and dangerous. There are always going to be obstacles in your path and detours to take, but it should never deter you from choosing to take that first courageous step for reclaiming your Happy Brain. After all, my motto is: *Happiness isn't a destination; it's a direction*. Thank you for allowing me to be your Happiness professor and for trusting me to be your guide on this empowering journey we all are on in order to forge a Happy Brain and a happy world. *It's time we try; it's time we tribe.*

Lastly, here is my final blessing to you: *Never be afraid to let your light and happiness shine forth fully and brightly, for the world would be a much dimmer place without you in it.*

Bonus Content

You may have personal anecdotes that seem small and inconsequential at the time, but I invite you to share them. Visit www.ScienceofaHappyBrain.com and social media channels to share content and material for helping your friends, family, co-workers, and neighbors develop the strategy for a Happy Brain, happy life, and happy world. Most importantly, I personally wish for you to become part of our movement and advance our effort to reclaim and restore our power to tribe. The world needs you. Happy.

EPILOGUE

HAPPINESS AND THE GREAT AMERICAN EXPERIMENT

> To be connected to America's causes—liberty, equal justice, respect for the dignity of all people—brings happiness more sublime than life's fleeting pleasures. Our identities and sense of worth are not circumscribed but enlarged by serving good causes bigger than ourselves.
>
> —Senator John McCain

As I reflect writing this final piece, the nation mourns the passing of one of its modern-day heroes, Senator John McCain. Whether or not you agreed with his politics, what made Sen. McCain's death and funeral an emotional touchstone for me and many Americans is the testament to the integrity of the person and to the embodiment of his patriotism in service to our country. Personally, how I'll remember Sen. McCain is someone who deeply understood the concept of happiness in the context of the "Great American Experiment" and the crucial crossroads where our democracy stands. Allow me to explain.

In January 1790 America's first president, George Washington, wrote in a letter the following: "The establishment of our new Government seemed to be the last great experiment for promoting human happiness by reasonable compact in civil society." For Washington, Jefferson, Franklin, and the Founding Fathers (and

Mothers) of the United States, American democracy was a radically social and political experiment for its time. Established upon the bold principles of liberty, self-governance, and independence, many noted figures instrumental in the birth of America were skeptical of this risky, novel form of governance known as American democracy.

Despite nearly two hundred and fifty years of wars, massive civil unrest, social upheaval, and political turmoil, the Great American Experiment still remains strong. Yet, something is currently erupting within our democracy that has the potential to jeopardize the nature and the direction of the experiment. The Great American Experiment can progress in two diverging directions—each established on the two competing visions of what defines happiness and who in America gets to benefit from this ideal construct of happiness. Through the lens of my research in brain science and behavioral health, these two visions of American happiness reflect the two competing aspects of your Stone-Age Tribe brain and your Social Brain.

The tribalism or factionalism many pundits view that's splitting the fabric of our democracy isn't so much the clash between liberals and conservatives, rural and urban, rich and poor. It's the battle between the two evolutionary brains—the Stone-Age Tribe brain and the Social Brain. The first vision of American happiness is a collective expression of the primal Stone-Age Tribe brain's propensity toward strife, scarcity, and suspicion that can promote the hatred, fear, exclusion, and ugliness witnessed as tribalism. The second vision of American happiness is a reflection of the more evolved Social Brain's drive for caring, inclusion, nurturing, compassion, and solidarity. From the perspective of evolutionary biology and human behavior, both views respectively are valid and can be justified.

At the heart of this cultural, social, political, and ideological "civil war" that's rapidly boiling in America today exists a bitter battle among the two evolutionary expressions of the human brain. One side reflects the strong sentiment from those who want to slow down the experiment—those who view it's gone too far or it's accelerating too quickly that they find threatening. Those who fall into that camp represent the collective anxiety of the Stone-Age Tribe brain's drive for safety, security, and stability. On the other end, there are those who want to expand the boundaries of the experiment—to explore the inclusion of new social and cultural elements that they believe are essential for the Great American Experiment to thrive.

The future of American democracy rests upon the outcome of this timeless tug-of-war between the primal Stone-Age Tribe brain and the more evolved Social Brain. To those Americans who want to limit or dissolve the Great American Experiment, the right to "Life, Liberty, and the pursuit of Happiness" is granted only upon a specific, chosen group of Americans they perceive to be part of their own tribe. For other Americans who desire to expand or reinvent the Great American Experiment, happiness is extended and open to anyone who qualifies and warrants the right to be part of our "American" tribe. The solution to our national turmoil resides in the reconciliation of the universal human struggle between the Stone-Age Tribe brain and the Social Brain.

Many Americans past and present, including Sen. McCain, cleverly realize these concepts. The success and longevity of the Great American Experiment happens by remembering what unites us as Americans, rather than focus on what divides us as a nation. Although Sen. McCain never uttered the phrase "The Great American Experiment," his distinguished life and noted career testify to its very essence embodied in his own words—*to live one's life in service to a cause, a purpose, or an ideal bigger than oneself is the greatest source of happiness.*

Dedicating your life to this cause, this purpose, this ideal bigger than yourself that delivers the greatest source of happiness is the Great American Experiment. The Great American Experiment is about happiness—the happiness of "We the People of the United States, in Order to form a more perfect Union," as stated in the Declaration of Independence. The reconciliation of these polarizing expressions of your Stone-Age Tribe brain and of your Social Brain rampant today is the "more perfect Union" that permeates the soul of American democracy.

When drafting the Declaration of Independence, the Founding Fathers affirmed why the "pursuit of Happiness" isn't just a principle to be pursued individually, but one we strive for as a society. That's right, happiness spans the self and society. Yet, America and American democracy are at a perilous point. The Disease of Despair raging today is intimately related to America's deeper existential crisis of identity. We're a nation in the midst of collectively redefining "The American Dream" and revisioning the Great American Experiment. Alluding to the recent book by American historian Jon Meacham, we're witnessing the healing of "The Soul of America." The Great American Experiment is fundamentally to heal the heart and soul of American happiness.

In this politically divisive time we currently find ourselves in, it's important to remember that happiness isn't a partisan issue. The right to a Happy Brain isn't exclusive to only one social group, political party, religion, or ethnicity. In fact, if we're to alleviate society's Disease of Despair, it requires the collective effort and commitment of all members of society—liberals, conservatives, independents, rich, poor, White, Black, Latino, Asian, LGBT, Christian, Jew, Muslim, Buddhist, Hindu, rural, urban people, and more. It basically requires all members of our American Tribe.

I have to admit the original direction of *Science of a Happy Brain* started off more as a "self-help" guide exploring how brain science research can be applied to assist individuals to experience greater balance, longevity, and resilience in life. Along the way, I had a profound revelation: *Science of a Happy Brain* acts as a social commentary. When envisioning this book in early 2017, two crucial factors were revealed to me that ultimately shaped this current work. They both exemplify how the emerging science of happiness and the power of tribe bear relevance that spans the domains of politics, public policy, and social medicine, while also intimately relating to your own personal quest for a Happy Brain.

The first was the tumultuous and contentious 2016 American election that exposed a deep-seated level of national strife and unmasked a disturbing level of social discontent and despair. The other was a noteworthy cross-cultural, long-term study presented in a conference at the London School of Economics (LSE) in December of 2016. Looking at this LSE study for the moment, it illuminates why the primary focus of economic and governmental strategy needs to be initiating policies geared around not just promoting economic prosperity, but also social health and collective well-being.

Why are these two events interconnected and relevant? The lead-up to and aftermath from the USA 2016 election, along with the research from the LSE conference, led me to two primary points for *Science of a Happy Brain*. The first underscores why individual happiness is intimately driven by your primal human need to feel a sense of value, belonging, and engagement with your tribe—a concept advanced by brain science and evolutionary psychology. The second affirms how the path for a prosperous and peaceful society is built not just on increasing individual happiness, but societal happiness.

In order for any nation to prosper and for its citizens to thrive, governmental policies need to be positioned around simultaneously advancing both a Happy Brain for you and others. One intention behind my life's work is to reveal why the science of happiness is one whose focus spans self and society, as their common goal is in framing the Happy Brain as the promotion of happiness not just for you, but for all.

Turning now to our national politics, what many political experts, policy wonks in Washington, D.C., and pundits in the media largely ignored in their analysis to explain the outcome of the USA 2016 election has to do with a prominent theory from brain science and evolutionary psychology—the Social Brain. Yet under times of strife and uncertainty, you can instinctively default to your primal survival needs for safety, security, and stability. In times of fear and perceived scarcity, you can operate from your Stone-Age Tribe brain—an undeniable vestige of human evolution—that reverts you back to the human developmental stage of strife, struggle, and suspicion. This primal expression of your Stone-Age Tribe brain is what reinforces the "us versus them" mentality of tribalism witnessed in our politics and society today.

Just to remember, tribalism isn't the same as tribe. Tribalism is associated with your Stone-Age Tribe brain; tribe is a product of your Social Brain. The Social Brain is what allowed humans the ability to become the dominant species on the planet. Although one positive aspect of your Stone-Age Tribe brain allowed your ancient ancestors to band together for survival during times of hardship, there's an ugly downside. Just as the cognitive frame of your Stone-Age Tribe brain prioritizes the happiness for those whom you believe to be "in your tribe," it can justify the active denial of happiness for those you deem to be "outside your tribe." Your desire for a Happy Brain shouldn't come at the expense of denying happiness to another or to an entire social group. Happiness isn't binary nor exclusionary. In other words, happiness isn't a zero-sum concept—the happiness for those you perceive to be "in your tribe" doesn't rob the right to happiness for those you view "outside your tribe."

Tribalism—the "us versus them" view of the world—is the negative outcome of your Stone-Age Tribe brain, which at its worst perpetuates social division and critically acts as an impediment to advance your Happy Brain for you and society. Understanding the consequences when an entire social group operates from its collective Stone-Age Tribe brain provides a novel approach into the outcome of the 2016 USA election. It similarly explains the 2016 Brexit referendum, along with the disturbing rise of nationalism, xenophobia, and religious fundamentalism occurring in the world. While pundits often view these as expressions of tribalism, the deeper culprit is the Stone-Age Tribe brain.

As someone who investigates the brain science of human behavior and received my master's degree in international political economics, please permit me to go on the record to state how in both of these 2016 electoral events—the Brexit referendum and USA election—the Stone-Age Tribe brain is the hidden factor at play. When a segment of a population experiences a lack of belonging or reports feeling somehow abandoned by the greater tribe of society at large, or claims its cultural, religious, ethnic, or social identity is under threat, the consequential result is a low sense of life-satisfaction within the "perceived" marginalized group.

The second core concept comes from behavioral science and public policy, illustrated by the conclusions reached from the LSE landmark study. The report states the key factor that determines happiness, both for self and society, is the degree to which governments and communities recognize and address the criteria that diminish social dissatisfaction and promote well-being. With all things being equal, the one factor that would reduce suffering and misery for individuals, and thereby for society, isn't resolved only by raising income or job-creation (although they are needed). Rather, it's in simultaneously implementing programs and strategies as public policy to curtail depression, addiction, mental illness, and anxiety that manifest as society's Disease of Despair. From the perspective of brain science and human behavior, securing the success of the Great American Experiment necessitates the collective advancement and application of the four Happiness Strategies of Biological Comfort, Psychological Contribution, Social Connection, and Spiritual Compassion.

Here's why the implications of the Social Brain model and the necessity for tribe are important: They have direct applications not just for your individual well-being, but they equally and powerfully address solutions that impact society at large. As Thomas Jefferson once famously penned, "The care of human life and happiness... is the only legitimate object of good government." It comes as no surprise that Jefferson and other American Founding Fathers would advance such an idea, as it aligns directly to the original notion of your Happy Brain.

When a government's public policy focuses on both creating "wealth and well-being" for its citizenry, it establishes the foundation for a resilient society. Countries such as the Himalayan nation of Bhutan already recognize the importance of happiness as an economic issue. It became the first country back in the 1970s to initiate and integrate Gross National Happiness as part of governmental policy. Other nations, such as the United Kingdom, France, and the United Arab Emirates have created government policy or have ministers dedicated to making happiness a social, political, and economic priority. Even the former UK Prime Minister David Cameron admits, "The country would be better off if we thought about well-being as well as economic growth." If a government truly cares and values its citizens, it will have to implement national policies that advance the science of a Happy Brain for all its citizens—not just for a specific segment of the electorate.

While *Science of a Happy Brain* can stand alone as a self-help piece on how to achieve greater happiness in your life—as many books in the genre do—my intention is to push beyond those boundaries. What makes this work unique is that it provides an opportunity for you to recognize why personal happiness cannot be examined in isolation from societal happiness. How can we thrive collectively as a "global tribe" when entire sectors of society and millions of your fellow human citizens are merely trying to survive?

As part of my research and exploration for this book, I've traveled across this amazing country and spoken to people from all walks of life. In June 2018 I launched this project in Lambertville, New Jersey—a small community tucked away on the Delaware River on the border of Pennsylvania. My decision to make Lambertville the inaugural debut for *Science of a Happy Brain* is embodied in the town's motto: "Lambertville is about Neighbor helping Neighbor." Those six simple words describe the quintessential tribute to tribe and strategy for your Happy Brain. Rural farmers, former urbanites, mill workers, single working moms, gay couples, grandparents, the wealthy, the working class, Democrats, Republicans, and people from all races co-exist to make Lambertville a desirable place to live. Lambertville is a testament to the Great American Experiment.

The key to your Happy Brain and to the Great American Experiment resides in your Social Brain. If you do nothing, your Stone-Age Tribe rules, tribalism and fear win, democracy dies, and the Great American Experiment ends. This dark shadow of tribe is grounded in the fear of believing that those "outside your tribe" will annihilate your sense of personal identity or established worldview. When tribalism is on the rise, it's all the more urgent why you learn the tools that empower you to operate from your more evolved Social Brain. In the words of another revered American statesman, Abraham Lincoln, "We are not enemies, but friends. We must not be enemies. Though passion may have strained, it must not break our bonds of affection. The mystic chords of memory will swell when again touched, as surely they will be, by the better angels of our nature." Lincoln's "better angels of our nature" is your Social Brain that seeks happiness for all and that resides at the core of the Great American Experiment.

In order for this Great American Experiment to continue and to succeed, it requires tending to the roots of American democracy and healing the existential pain that afflicts our nation's soul. Not necessarily reverting back to a glorified or romanticized period in American history but returning to America's core values and ideals, what Sen. McCain referred to as "liberty, equal justice, [and] respect for the dignity of all people." It's precisely what your Social Brain desires. If there's one thing I'm certain of, it's this: We're all driven in our shared goal for happiness. I genuinely want every one of you to enjoy the benefits of your Happy Brain by applying the tools you've acquired over the last ten lessons into your life. Together, I know each of you holds a valuable piece and plays a pivotal role in the unfolding of happiness and the Great American Experiment. United as a tribe, we make the world happy for all. It starts with your Happy Brain.

September 1, 2018
Dr. Jay Kumar
Your Happiness Professor

ABOUT THE AUTHOR

Jay Kumar, PhD (your Happiness professor), is a renowned public speaker and thought leader, whose expertise spans brain science, behavioral health, economics, politics, culture, and religion. He holds a master's degree in international political economy from Columbia University's School of International and Public Affairs. Over the years, Dr. Jay has shared his powerful insights and proven strategies for happiness with hundreds of university students, thousands of radio listeners, and vast audiences throughout the US and internationally. He is also the author of *Brain, Body & Being*, and is frequently featured in media stories revealing how to overcome life's challenges and to tap into the inner power and innate potential for your Happy Brain. Dr. Jay's latest initiative—*America's State of Mind*—is a media platform that explores the dynamic intersection of science, spirituality, and society in order to identify the sources and advance solutions for critical issues facing our contemporary and complex world. Join Dr. Jay's "Happiness Tribe" and benefit from inspiring interviews, informative conversations, latest research, and empowering daily lessons for your Happy Brain on Facebook, Twitter, and Instagram (@docjaykumar). Learn more at www.DrJayKumar.com.

CPSIA information can be obtained
at www.ICGtesting.com
Printed in the USA
FFHW021910021219
56538656-62337FF